PSALMS *and* PROVERBS *for* EVERYDAY LIFE

100 Daily Devotions

JOEL OSTEEN

New York • Nashville

RULE YOUR DAY
Rule Your Day Journal

THE POWER OF FAVOR
The Power of Favor Study Guide

THE POWER OF I AM
The Power of I Am Journal
The Power of I Am Study Guide
Daily Readings from The Power of I Am

THINK BETTER, LIVE BETTER
Think Better, Live Better Journal
Think Better, Live Better Study Guide
Daily Readings from Think Better, Live Better

WITH VICTORIA OSTEEN
Our Best Life Together
Wake Up to Hope Devotional

YOU ARE STRONGER THAN YOU THINK
You Are Stronger than You Think Study Guide

YOU CAN, YOU WILL
You Can, You Will Journal
Daily Readings from You Can, You Will

YOUR BEST LIFE NOW
Your Best Life Begins Each Morning
Your Best Life Now for Moms
Your Best Life Now Journal
Your Best Life Now Study Guide
Daily Readings from Your Best Life Now
Scriptures and Meditations for Your Best Life Now
Starting Your Best Life Now

YOUR GREATER IS COMING
Your Greater Is Coming Study Guide

PSALMS *and*
PROVERBS
for
EVERYDAY LIFE

FaithWords

Hachette Book Group

1290 Avenue of the Americas, New York, NY 10104

faithwords.com

twitter.com/faithwords

First Edition: November 2023

FaithWords is a division of Hachette Book Group, Inc. The FaithWords name and logo are trademarks of Hachette Book Group, Inc.

The publisher is not responsible for websites (or their content) that are not owned by the publisher.

FaithWords books may be purchased in bulk for business, educational, or promotional use. For information, please contact your local bookseller or the Hachette Book Group Special Markets Department at special.markets@hbgusa.com.

Literary development: Lance Wubbels Literary Services, Bloomington, Minnesota.

Library of Congress Cataloging-in-Publication Data has been applied for.

ISBN: 9781546005285 (hardcover), 9781546005292 (ebook)

Printed in the United States of America

LSC-C

Printing 1, 2023

CONTENTS

INTRODUCTION

My favorite way to start the day is with prayer and worship and by reading God's Word. My parents taught me and my brother and sisters the importance of spending time with God from our early teen years and showed us how to do it by their own example. This practice of beginning my day focused on God and His Word has made a profound impact on my life. Scripture tells us that His thoughts are higher than our thoughts and His ways are higher than our ways, which is why it is so important that we prioritize time to learn to hear what God thinks about us and what His Word says about us.

When our parents gave us our first Bible, they encouraged us to read daily from the book of Psalms and from the book of Proverbs. Psalms is a book full of encouragement and helps us maintain an attitude of worship toward God. Proverbs is called "the book of wisdom." It gives us practical advice and insight for everyday living. If you are like me, I need to be encouraged, and I need the wisdom of God daily. These are the reasons I wrote this devotional for you. As you read through this book, allow God to speak to you, to encourage you, and to impart His wisdom into your life. After you read the daily passage and prayer, continue to meditate on the thought and Scripture throughout the day. I know from experience that you will be greatly encouraged.

PSALMS *and* PROVERBS
for
EVERYDAY LIFE

TODAY'S SCRIPTURE

That person is like a tree planted by streams of water, which yields its fruit in season and whose leaf does not wither—whatever they do prospers.

PSALM 1:3 NIV

AN EXTRAORDINARY LIFE

The best decision of your life was to live your life with God at the center. That was the essential first step to living at your full potential. Now the key to experiencing an extraordinary life every day is to grow in your relationship with God. Scripture talks about how life with God is like a tree and its branches. When a branch is connected to the tree, it receives nourishment and life and produces fruit. We have to stay connected to God so we can receive His strength and be empowered to accomplish all that He has for us.

In any relationship, growth happens over time. God doesn't expect you to be perfect. He just wants you to keep moving forward with Him one step at a time. No matter what is going on in your life, keep making time for Him so that your relationship can grow strong and you can walk in the fullness of His blessings.

A PRAYER FOR TODAY

Father, thank You that every day I can live my life with You at the center and grow in my relationship with You. Thank You for planting me in the streams of Your living water. I look forward to the abundance You are producing in my life. In Jesus' name. Amen.

PRAY BOLD PRAYERS

In today's Scripture, God is saying, "I have nations for you. I have something awesome in your future, something bigger than you've imagined, but you have to ask." You're not going to see the nations, you're not going to see God do great things, if you're praying small, weak, limited prayers. There are dreams that God has put in your heart that you can't accomplish on your own. There are obstacles you'll face that are too big for you to overcome by yourself. If you don't learn to pray bold prayers, if you don't learn to ask God big, you'll get stuck where you are.

Bold prayers open doors you could never open and turn impossible situations around. When you pray boldly, you're releasing your faith. You're saying, "God, I know that You're the all-powerful Creator of the universe, that You can take me where I can't go on my own." Ask Him for what you want Him to do, ask Him for what you're believing for, ask Him today, and watch what God will do.

A PRAYER FOR TODAY

Father, thank You that the dreams You have put in my heart are always possible because no one is more powerful than You. Thank You that I can dare to pray big, to ask big, and to believe big. I believe that You have great things for me and are taking me where I could never go on my own. In Jesus' name. Amen.

USE THE POWER OF "BUT"

In today's Scripture, David was saying, "God, my enemies are multiplying." He not only had other armies trying to stop him, but his own son Absalom was trying to take the kingdom from him. David could have thought, *I can handle people from the outside trying to take me down, but now it's my own son. I'm done.* This could have been David's end. But after David stated the hard facts, he took it one step further and said, "But You, O Lord, are my shield." Notice that David added the "but." "I'm having a lot of trouble, but the Lord is my shield."

What's the message? Don't let the enemy have the last word. Always add the "but." "The medical report doesn't look good, but the Lord is my healer." "A coworker did me wrong, but God is fighting my battles." "I went through a loss, but God has beauty for ashes." Every time something negative happens, answer back with a "but."

A PRAYER FOR TODAY

Father, thank You for being a shield about me, my glory and the lifter of my head. Thank You that the enemy doesn't have the last word when something negative happens to me. I will use the power of "but" and see Your promises come to pass. In Jesus' name. Amen.

FEED YOUR DESTINY

Though we may not realize it, we're always feeding ourselves. What we watch and listen to, the people we're around, and the thoughts we're dwelling on are feeding our inner man. If you go to lunch with coworkers who feed you gossip, jealousy, and disrespect, before long you'll be gossiping, jealous, and critical. Whatever you feed on is going to grow. If you're always feeding on negative thoughts, thinking, *I'll never get out of debt, or get the job I want, or meet the right person*, you're feeding doubt, fear, and mediocrity.

Start feeding your faith, your hopes, your dreams. Your diet needs to be what God says about you. "I am

7

fearfully and wonderfully made. I am a masterpiece, made in the image of Almighty God." When you feed on God's values, your value will get stronger. Stay on your diet. No more feeding doubt, fear, and offense. No more hanging around the wrong people. Keep feeding your destiny.

A PRAYER FOR TODAY

Father, thank You for the provision of Your Word and all the nourishment and strength I receive from it. Help me to guard what I'm watching and listening to and to be careful with my relationships. I want to put my energies into my destiny. In Jesus' name. Amen.

*I am not afraid of ten thousand enemies
who surround me on every side.*

PSALM 3:6 NLT

WHEN YOU'RE SURROUNDED

You would think that being surrounded by ten thousand enemies would have David feeling worried, afraid, and upset. But he went on to say, "Victory comes from You, O Lord." He was saying, "I could be overwhelmed by my enemies, but I'm not falling apart because I know that God is surrounding what's surrounding me." David saw his enemies, but through his spiritual eyes he also saw the Most High God fighting his battles.

As with David, you may feel surrounded by enemies— depression, sickness, lack, obstacles. You don't have the people connections or the finances. You could easily accept it and think, *It's not meant to be.* Here is the key: What you see with your physical eyes is not the only thing that's surrounding you. If you open your eyes of faith, you'll realize the troubles and the opposition are surrounded by our God. You're not just surrounded by the negative. That's one level, but the all-powerful God supersedes that. You're surrounded by favor, surrounded by healing, and surrounded by angels.

A PRAYER FOR TODAY

Father, thank You that no matter what troubles I face, I can stay in peace knowing that You are surrounding every trouble and every opposing situation that's surrounding me. Help me to see with eyes of faith. I declare that I am surrounded by You, and You will bring me through to victory. In Jesus' name. Amen.

TODAY'S SCRIPTURE

*You have freed me when I was hemmed in
and enlarged me when I was in distress;
have mercy upon me and hear my prayer.*

PSALM 4:1 AMPC

ENLARGED

In today's Scripture, the psalmist David didn't say, "God enlarged me in my good times." He says, "God enlarged me when I faced a giant, when King Saul was trying to kill me, when my own father didn't believe in me." It was only in those times of adversity that David discovered talent, courage, favor, and greatness he didn't know he had.

You may be in the midst of adversity now, thinking, *God, what's going on in my life? This trouble is setting me back.* No, it's setting you up. What you can't see is that God is enlarging you. You're going to see new growth, new opportunities, new talent. It couldn't happen without the fire. There's favor coming in that distress, there's promotion in that challenge, there's freedom in that pain. The adversity is opening up things that you would never have seen. Don't fight the difficulty; stay faithful in the fire. The right attitude is: *God, I don't like it, but I trust You. I know You're in control. You wouldn't have allowed this difficulty unless it is making me better.*

A PRAYER FOR TODAY

Father, thank You that no matter what the difficulty is, You are worthy of my trust. Thank You that in the midst of adversity You are enlarging me and making me better. I believe that I am going to discover talent and courage that I didn't know I had. In Jesus' name. Amen.

KEEP YOUR COOL

God made us as emotional beings. All through the day you will feel things, but just because you feel something doesn't mean you have to act on it. You may feel anger, which is okay, but don't lose your temper. Keep your cool. You may feel offended, but don't give in to it. You may feel tempted to compromise when your flesh says, "I have to have it, the feeling is so strong," but you don't have to get on board with that feeling.

The flesh wants to control your life. You think you can't control it, but God wouldn't tell us to be angry and not give in if we couldn't do it. The feelings are real. You have to ask yourself, "If I follow what I'm feeling, is it going to move me toward my destiny? Is it going to help me improve? Or is it just my fleshly, carnal desires that are trying to keep me from rising higher?"

A PRAYER FOR TODAY

Father, thank You that one of the fruits of the Spirit working in me is self-control. Thank You that I don't have to be a slave to feelings that have tried to control me for years. I believe that I have the power to overcome, to say no to the flesh, and to be disciplined to do the right thing. In Jesus' name. Amen.

THE "I DON'T UNDERSTAND IT" FILE

Sometimes it's best to leave things alone. As long as you're probing around your hurts and disappointments, trying to figure out why something happened, you're never going to heal. You have to let it go and say, "God, I don't understand it, but I'm not going to keep trying to figure it out. I know that You wouldn't allow it if You couldn't bring good out of it, so I'm going to leave it with You."

You should have a file in your thinking called "I Don't Understand It." When things come up that don't make sense and you can't find an answer, instead of trying to figure it out, getting confused and frustrated, just put it in your "I Don't Understand It" file and move forward. If you make the mistake of going through life trying to figure out why something bad happened, why something didn't work out, why your prayer wasn't answered, that's going to poison your life.

A PRAYER FOR TODAY

Father, thank You that I can be free from trying to figure everything out on my own. I recognize that You wouldn't allow it in my life if You couldn't bring good out of it. I will place these matters in my "I Don't Understand It" file and move forward. In Jesus' name. Amen.

TODAY'S SCRIPTURE

In the morning, LORD, you hear my voice;
in the morning I lay my requests before
you and wait expectantly.

PSALM 5:3 NIV

PRAY WITH EXPECTANCY

Notice that in today's Scripture David didn't just pray and say, "Okay, God, I did my part." He prayed and then waited with expectation. He had his hopes up. He went through the day looking for God's goodness, talking like it was going to happen. He expected God's favor. He said, "Surely goodness and mercy will follow me everywhere I go."

When you pray, you have to follow it up with expectancy, with a knowing that the Creator of the universe has gone to work because He is a faithful God. What He promised you, He will bring to pass. You may have been waiting for a long time, but down in your spirit you have to have a resolve, a confidence: "I know the answer is on the way. I know the miracle is in motion. I've asked according to God's will. I know He's heard me. It's just a matter of time before it shows up."

A PRAYER FOR TODAY

Father, thank You that everything You've promised me will be released in my life because You are faithful. Thank You that You hear my prayers and that the answers are on the way. I am looking for Your goodness and believing that a miracle has been set in motion. In Jesus' name. Amen.

Surely, LORD, you bless the righteous; you surround them with your favor as with a shield.

PSALM 5:12 NIV

SURROUNDED BY FAVOR

When we receive a promotion, or meet someone special, or the medical report turns around, we know that's the favor of God. But when we face challenges and things are coming against us, it doesn't seem as though we have favor. But having favor doesn't mean you won't have obstacles; favor is what keeps those challenges from defeating you. Today's Scripture says that God's favor is surrounding you in the good times and the tough times.

The psalmist says, "I have anointed him. I will steady him and make him strong. His enemies shall not overpower him." In the middle of that challenge you need to remind yourself that you are anointed and crowned with favor. Right now God is steadying you, making you strong, pushing back the forces of darkness, and taking you to victory. You know a secret: You are surrounded with His favor in the storm, and God is turning the challenge to your advantage.

A PRAYER FOR TODAY

Father, thank You that You have put Your favor upon me and that it surrounds me like a shield at all times. Thank You that I am crowned with favor and that You are steadying me and strengthening me and leading me to victory over every challenge. I will trust You in the good times and the tough times. In Jesus' name. Amen.

HOLD ON TO
YOUR CROWN

When God breathed His life into you, He put a crown of glory and honor on your head. This crown represents your authority. It represents God's blessing and favor on your life. It's a reminder that you are royalty, a child of the Most High God. You're not ordinary; you're extraordinary because He breathed His life into you. When you're wearing your crown, you'll have a sense of entitlement, thinking, *I have a right to be blessed and live in victory because I'm wearing a crown of honor put there by my Creator.*

Jesus said, "Hold on to what you have, so that no one will take your crown." Throughout life, there will always be someone or something trying to take your crown. People will talk about you, trying to make you look bad, to push you down. What they're really doing is trying to take your crown. Don't let them have it. Nobody can take your crown. You have to let go of what was said or done to you rather than let go of your crown.

A PRAYER FOR TODAY

Father, thank You that You have put a crown of glory and honor on my head by Your grace. Thank You that I am not less than others or just average, but You have made me royalty. I declare I will not allow anyone or anything to take my crown. In Jesus' name. Amen.

*In everything you do, put God first,
and he will direct you and crown
your efforts with success.*

PROVERBS 3:6 TLB

PUT GOD FIRST

A lot of people are good at taking care of the physical and emotional parts of their lives, but they don't take care of the spiritual. There's minimal or no connection to God.

Your life will be more fulfilling when you're in relationship with your Creator. He breathed life into you. He knows what your purpose is. He wants to give you the advantage for success. When you make Him a part of your life, His favor will take you where your talents and abilities can't.

Make your spiritual life a priority. When you get up in the morning, take time to thank God for the day. Don't run out of the house stressed out, in a hurry. Start the day off with a grateful attitude. Read the Scripture, meditate on His promises, and fill your mind with thoughts of faith, hope, and victory. Put God first, and He will crown your efforts with success.

A PRAYER FOR TODAY

Father, thank You that You invited me into a relationship with You. I want, in everything I do, to put You first and have You direct my life. Thank You for speaking to me through Your Word. I believe that You will crown my efforts with success. In Jesus' name. Amen.

THE GOD WHO OVERRULES

In the legal system, a court will rule on a case and give its verdict, but that verdict can be appealed to a higher court that has more authority and can overrule what the lower court decided. Finally, the Supreme Court has the highest authority, and it can overrule any lower court decision.

In today's Scripture, the psalmist is saying that the enemies that come against you—the fear, the lack, the sickness, the addiction—are not permanent. Our God is called the Most High God. He is the Supreme Court all by Himself. God is about to rule in your favor. He's about to overrule some things. You're about to get a new verdict. God is about to turn some things around. You're going to see a breakthrough in your health. Doors are going to open wider than you've imagined. God is going to bring divine connections, the right people. He's going to thrust you to a new level of your destiny.

A PRAYER FOR TODAY

Father, thank You for being the God who has the authority and power to overrule the negative things in my life that seem permanent. Thank You that You are ruling in my favor. I believe I'm stepping into freedom, wholeness, and a new level of my destiny. In Jesus' name. Amen.

IN HIS PRESENCE

Sometimes we get up in the morning and think, *I don't feel like reading my Bible today. I'm too tired to pray.* But once you develop the habit and see the benefits of how you feel refreshed and restored, make better decisions, and have God's favor, you'll think, *I can't afford not to do this.* Spending time with God is that vital to living a victorious life.

Today's Scripture says that in God's presence there is fullness of joy, fullness of peace, fullness of victory. That's where you're refreshed and restored. Take time to invest in your spiritual well-being by sitting quietly in God's presence, praying, and reading your Bible. When you get alone with God, the rest of your day will go much better. All through the day, meditate on God's promises. Put on some good praise music. Put God first and you won't be able to contain all the good things He will bring across your path.

A PRAYER FOR TODAY

Father, thank You that I can come into Your presence right now because Jesus has made a way for me. Thank You for the privilege of spending time with You and reading Your Word. Speak to my heart and show me the path for my life, and I will run to follow You. In Jesus' name. Amen.

You armed me with strength for battle;
you humbled my adversaries before me.

PSALM 18:39 NIV

FULLY ARMED

Why don't you start out your day with an image of victory? You're not weak, defeated, or overcome by problems. You're a warrior. You've been armed with strength for every battle. You're full of can-do power. The forces for you are greater than the forces against you. Don't go through life magnifying the wrong things, causing you to see yourself as small or limited. Don't think the problem is too big, that you can't overcome a sickness, get out of debt, or break an addiction. The reason the enemy is trying to distort your image is because he knows who you really are. He knows you're a giant killer. He knows you're made in the image of God. He knows you have seeds of greatness. Don't let his lies keep you from step-ping into your greatness. Don't let a wrong self-image keep you from leaving your mark. How much further will you go, how much happier will you live, how much more confidence will you have, if you get rid of the dis-torted images and start seeing yourself the way God sees you?

A PRAYER FOR TODAY

Father, thank You for arming me with strength for every battle that I will ever face. Thank You that You have already equipped me with power as a warrior and destined me for victory. I declare that I am strong and can do all things through Christ. In Jesus' name. Amen.

IT'S IN YOUR POWER

The reason some people in your life are not reaching their potential is that they're lacking nourishment. They need someone to speak words of faith into them. Many times you can see things in people that they can't see in themselves. You have what they need. If you encourage them, let them know that you believe in them, call out their seeds of greatness, you'll see them come to life. Gifts will come out that they didn't know they had. Their passion will come back. Before long, they'll be stepping into new levels. It wasn't something they could do on their own. They needed your kind words of nourishment to their soul.

This is something that we can all do. In twenty seconds, you can give someone a compliment. You can send a text or make a call. "I'm thinking about you. I appreciate your friendship. You're really amazing." You have it in your power to do. Live your life as a healer, be free with kind words to lift people, to speak life to their dreams, to tell them what they can become.

A PRAYER FOR TODAY

Father, thank You for what You've brought me through that I can now use to nourish others. Thank You that I have something to give, some blessing to impart, to help make their dreams come true. I want to be a healer and use my words to lift others. In Jesus' name. Amen.

*Some trust in chariots and some in horses,
but we trust in the name of the LORD our God.*

PSALM 20:7 NIV

SET YOUR MIND ON TRUST

In modern times, today's Scripture would say, "Some trust in money and some in their job. Some trust in what the economists say, but we trust in the God who created it all. He's called Jehovah Jireh, 'the Lord our provider.'" When you meditate on that, you won't have fear. You'll have peace and be at rest. You know God is in control, and He can give you victory. But it all depends on what's going on in your thought life. You can meditate on the problem or you can meditate on the promises.

Meditating on the problem doesn't make it better; it makes it worse.

If you don't set your mind on trusting God, the enemy will set it for you. He will remind you of how bad you have it, how many mistakes you've made, all the people who have come against you, and on and on. Your life is going to follow your thoughts.

A PRAYER FOR TODAY

Father, thank You that You are Jehovah Jireh, the Lord my provider. Thank You that I can set my trust in You completely rather than in what the world tells me to trust in. I believe and declare that You give me peace, and I will rest in You in all the circumstances of my life. In Jesus' name. Amen.

For you have given him his heart's desire;
you have withheld nothing he requested.

PSALM 21:2 NLT

YOUR HEART'S DESIRES

We all have dreams we've given up on. Too often we think it's been too long, we've made too many mistakes, the problem will never turn around, and we accept that it's always going to be this way. But just because it hasn't happened yet doesn't mean it's not going to happen. Who told you that you're not going to love again, not going to be healthy again, or not going to get the house loan? That didn't come from God. It may feel like it's over, but God is saying, "I'm still going to bring that dream to pass."

Now you have to get in agreement with God and start expecting again.

As long as you think it will never work out, that's going to keep you from the new things God has in store. Don't believe those lies. Start dreaming again, start believing again. Freedom is in your future. Wholeness belongs to you. Get your passion back. Stir up your gifts. What God promised you He's still going to bring to pass.

A PRAYER FOR TODAY

Father, thank You for the expectancy rising in my heart that You have good things in store for me. Thank You that my hopes and dreams can be in You alone. I believe and declare that nothing is going to keep me from what You have in store. In Jesus' name. Amen.

TODAY'S SCRIPTURE

O My God, I cry in the daytime,
but You do not hear; and in the night
season, and am not silent.

PSALM 22:2 NKJV

TIMES OF SILENCE

To get to where God is taking you, to the amazing future He has planned, requires that you trust Him in times of silence, when there's no sign that He's working. If you have to see everything to stay encouraged and keep believing, it will limit how high you will go. You have to pass the test of staying in faith and thanking God when it feels as though He is on vacation and isn't even hearing your prayers.

The silence doesn't mean God has forgotten about you. He sees your faithfulness. He sees you doing the right thing when it's hard. When you could have given up, you kept believing and praising. Every thought said it was never going to happen, but you kept thanking God that He was working. Your time is coming. What God promised is on the way. Don't let people, delays, or doubts convince you to give up. Your breakthrough is already on the schedule. Your miracle has already been set in motion. Get ready. What you're believing for is going to happen suddenly, unexpectedly.

A PRAYER FOR TODAY

Father, thank You for the good plan You have for my life. Even when I don't understand things, even when You seem to be silent, I choose to put my hope and trust in You. I believe that my time is coming and that what You have promised is on the way. In Jesus' name. Amen.

*Above all else, guard your heart,
for everything you do flows from it.*

PROVERBS 4:23 NIV

GUARD YOUR HEART

One of our most important responsibilities is to keep our heart pure. It's easy to let what's on the outside get inside. It takes discipline to say, "I'm not going to dwell on that offense. I'm not going to feel sorry for myself because something didn't work out." Maybe you need to forgive somebody, or maybe you're still sour about a dream that didn't work out, or maybe you're still beating yourself up over a mistake you made. You only have so much emotional energy each day. It's not an unlimited supply. Do you know how much energy it takes to hold a grudge, to go around offended? That's wasting valuable energy that you need for your dreams, for your children, and for your destiny.

Life is too short for you to live offended, not forgiving, bitter over what didn't work out. Quit letting what's on the outside get inside; start guarding your heart.

A PRAYER FOR TODAY

Father, thank You that I can guard my heart and keep it pure from all the negative things that try to enter in. I declare that I will not allow offenses to get inside. I want Your stream of grace to flow unhindered in and through my life. In Jesus' name. Amen.

YOU ARE ENOUGH

It's very powerful when you can say, "I have the talent I need. I have the looks I need. I have the personality I need. I have the strength I need." David had plenty of opportunities to live with a deficit mentality. Before he became the greatest king who ever lived, he was discounted by his father and his brothers. They made him feel as though he was unqualified, not good enough, and inferior. If David had relied on other people to get his approval, he would never have stepped into his destiny.

Maybe someone has discounted you and made you feel that you're not attractive enough, not talented enough, not up to par. Don't believe those lies. Those people didn't breathe life into you. They don't determine your destiny. Do as David did and say, "Father, thank You that I have everything I need in You." You don't need other people's approval or validation. The Most High God has approved you. He's the One who matters.

A PRAYER FOR TODAY

Father, thank You that You have given me every-thing I need to fulfill my purpose. Thank You that I am enough because You made me just as I am, and I have Your approval. I believe and declare that I am talented enough, I am attrac-tive enough, and I am strong enough. In Jesus' name. Amen.

LIVE BALANCED

The Scripture says that our body is the temple of the Holy Spirit and we must take care of it. You can't go against natural laws and expect God to bless you. Constant busyness and fatigue will make you feel flat.

It's easy to work all the time, to always be thinking about business, about some problem you must solve. That's doing yourself and the people around you a disservice. Your mind needs a break; your body needs to relax. That's why God required the people in the Old Testament to take a Sabbath. They had to rest.

If you live stressed out and overworked, don't eat right or sleep enough, eventually God will *make* you lie down in green pastures. You'll probably come to a point where you have to rest. Don't wear yourself out to the point that God has to make you slow down. You need recreation, exercise, and laughter. The key is to live balanced—physically, spiritually, and emotionally.

A PRAYER FOR TODAY

Father, thank You for giving me my body to live in and to care for as a temple of Your Spirit. Thank You that You made me to work and be productive as well as to rest and to laugh. Help me keep myself healthy and living a balanced life. In Jesus' name. Amen.

A BETTER WAY

When others are trying to make you look bad, it's easy to live upset, be mad at people, and think of the ways you can shut them down or get even. But that's not your job. Your job is to guard your heart. Don't let the offense, the bitterness, or the poison get inside. Do your part, and God will do His part. He'll take care of your reputation. He can cause you to shine in the face of what they're doing. Sometimes that's a bigger miracle.

We think, *God, just shut them up, change their mind, show them that they're wrong.* God says, "I have a better way. I'm going to prepare a feast for you and promote you while they're still talking. I'm going to lift you up while they're doing their best to push you down." In spite of someone's best attempts to make you look bad, you keep excelling, you keep growing, you keep smiling, you keep being good to people, you keep seeing favor and promotion. God knows how to take care of your reputation.

A PRAYER FOR TODAY

Father, thank You that You have Your ways of preparing feasts for me when I face opposition and critics. Thank You that You will take care of my reputation and that I don't need to live upset. I will guard my heart and keep the poison out. In Jesus' name. Amen.

Look straight ahead, and fix your eyes on what lies before you. Mark out a straight path for your feet; stay on the safe path.

PROVERBS 4:25–26 NLT

LOOK STRAIGHT AHEAD

You may have been hurt and have a reason to stay down and live bitter, but you don't have a right. God still has a great purpose in front of you. He saw what they did, who left you out, what you lost. He says He has beauty for those ashes. But you can't sit around nursing your wounds and asking, "Why me?" Don't put a question mark where God has put a period. Part of faith is trusting when life doesn't make sense. You're never going to understand every painful thing that happens. You can't let it sour the rest of your life. You have to get back up.

That means you quit reliving and thinking about the hurts. God knows how to make it up to you. When He sees you moving forward when you could be sitting in defeat, when you're being good to someone even though you've been through hurts, God is going to show out in your life. You will see greater favor because of the unfair things. God will turn it to your advantage.

A PRAYER FOR TODAY

Father, thank You that my life is in Your hands and that You have a great purpose for me. Thank You that the hurts and wounds that I don't understand now are going to be turned to my advantage. I believe that You are going to show out in my life in an even greater way. In Jesus' name. Amen.

Open up, ancient gates! Open up, ancient doors, and let the King of glory enter.

PSALM 24:7 NLT

OPEN THE ANCIENT GATES

Ancient gates are doors that have been shut for years, things you've been shut out of by lack, depression, low self-esteem, or mediocrity. Ancient gates are about to open up, and you're about to walk into blessings, freedom, wholeness, and new levels. Chains are breaking right now, deadbolt locks are coming off, and ancient doors are opening. What you couldn't make happen, the King of glory, the Most High God, your doorkeeper, will make happen. You're coming into a season of greater favor, greater opportunity, greater anointing, greater influence.

When you realize that God is your doorkeeper, you can live in peace. You can stay in faith, knowing that God will get you to where you're supposed to be. When the ancient gate is not moving, keep walking by faith. Keep telling every closed door, "You're not permanent. My doorkeeper has the final say." When it's the right time, it's going to open. You don't have to force it, manipulate the situation, or strive to make it happen. It will happen by the hand of God.

A PRAYER FOR TODAY

Father, thank You that there is no ancient door in my life that You can't open. Thank You that You are the doorkeeper, the King of glory, and that at the right time You'll take me through the things I don't understand. I declare that I will stay in faith and live in peace. In Jesus' name. Amen.

WHISPERED SECRETS

When you honor God, He'll tell you secrets. He'll whisper things in your spirit that you had no way of knowing. He knows when you need to spend time with someone for reasons of which you're completely unaware. He knows how to connect you with the right person at the right time. He knows where your best place is to work. He knows where the good breaks are, the promotion, the resources, the abundance. He'll give you inside information for your good. It's a gentle whisper, the secret of the Lord.

It won't always make sense. It may not seem logical. The facts may say otherwise. A battle will take place between your mind and the gentle whisper. When it's from God, it's more of a knowing. You can't explain it, but deep down you have this peace. You don't have any data to back it up, but you do have the Most High God living inside you. You know you're supposed to do it. Trust the whisper. Obey the promptings, the knowing, the still small voice. That's God whispering secrets.

A PRAYER FOR TODAY

Father, thank You for being my Lord and God and for always being there to lead and guide me in the way I should go. Thank You that You whisper secrets in my spirit and give me insight I couldn't know on my own. Help me to be sensitive to Your voice and just obey. In Jesus' name. Amen.

WALK IN INTEGRITY

We're living in a day when God is going to show out in new ways. He's looking for people, number one, who honor Him by living a life of integrity, of character, of keeping Him first place. We have to have integrity in our finances and relationships, in how we treat people, in what we watch. Integrity is the foundation that a successful life is built upon.

And number two, He's looking for people who believe big, who get out of their comfort zone and ask for things they cannot do on their own. That's when God steps in. When every circumstance says there's no way, that's when God says, "Let Me show you why I'm called 'the Great I Am.' Let Me show you who controls the universe, how I can open doors, how I can change people's minds, how I can cause the right people to show up, how I break chains that have held you back. Let Me show you how I bring favor, promotion, and influence that catapults you further than you could imagine."

A PRAYER FOR TODAY

Father, thank You for challenging me to make sure that integrity is the foundation of my life. Show me if there is anything I'm doing that is keeping me from being my best. I want You to show out as the Great I Am in my life in new ways and believe You to do more than I can imagine. In Jesus' name. Amen.

BE GENEROUS

Being a generous person is more than just being generous with your finances. There are people in your life right now with whom you need to be generous with words that assure them you love and believe in them. They need to hear you validate them over and over again. This should start with your family. Don't take for granted the people who are closest to you. You may think that they know you're proud of them. No, something happens when they hear you say it. Those kind words get down into their spirit and bring a new level of confidence, talent, and boldness.

There may be people in your life now with whom

you're not happy. It's easy to focus on how someone isn't measuring up, how they should be more disciplined and going further. Maybe all they need is some encouragement. Here's a key: Be generous with your compliments and encouragement. Be generous in telling them what you like about them and what they can do. You have the power to push them into their destiny.

A PRAYER FOR TODAY

Father, thank You for the people You have placed in my life and the special role You have given me in their lives. Thank You that You can take my words of encouragement and bring healing and cheer to them. Help me to see who I can bless and lift up today. In Jesus' name. Amen.

For he will conceal me there when troubles come;
he will hide me in his sanctuary.
He will place me out of reach on a high rock.

PSALM 27:5 NLT

WHY BE AFRAID?

David had all kinds of things come against him—people, armies, even his own family. He had many reasons to live worried, upset, and bitter. But he said, "The Lord is my light and my salvation—whom shall I fear? Why should I be afraid?" David lived with this attitude: *God's got this. I'm not going to worry or live in fear. He will hide me when trouble comes. He will place me out of reach.*

You may have discouraging situations and difficulties coming against you, but God has placed you out of reach. They can't defeat you. Now do as David did and remain confident. Keep your peace. You may feel like you're surrounded by an army, but the truth is that you're surrounded by God's favor. The forces for you are greater than the forces against you. God's got this. He's done it in the past, and He's not going to stop now.

A PRAYER FOR TODAY

Father, thank You that You are my light and my salvation and the stronghold of my life. Thank You for Your promise of protecting me when troubles come and placing me out of its reach. I will live from a place of peace, knowing I am safe in the palms of Your hands. In Jesus' name. Amen.

CHOSEN

In 1 Samuel 16, when the prophet Samuel came to David's house to anoint the next king of Israel, his father didn't bother to bring him in from the shepherds' fields. David's seven older brothers were bigger, stronger, talented, and good looking. He was discounted, forsaken, and pushed down even by his brothers. But God doesn't choose the way we choose. When David was brought in, God said, "David is the next king. I'm about to reverse the order. I'm taking David from the back to the front, from the least to the leader."

If our destiny depended only on who likes us, who believes in us, who thinks we're talented, we'd get stuck.

There will always be people who leave you out, forsake you, and try to hold you back. The good news is, they don't control your destiny. The Most High God is ordering your steps. He's working out His plan for your life. You keep doing the right thing, and vindication and respect will come knocking on your door. When it's your time, promotion will come looking for you.

A PRAYER FOR TODAY

Father, thank You that You see the greatness that is in me and that You alone control my destiny. When others don't give me their approval or affirm me, help me to let it go. I believe that Your approval is all that really matters, and I declare that You are unfolding Your plan for my life. In Jesus' name. Amen.

TURN THE PAGE

The Scripture talks about how God has written every day of our lives in His book. When we go through things that we don't understand, things that aren't fair, things that are painful, it's easy to get stuck on that page and think it's never going to change. Can I encourage you that it's just one chapter, not your whole book? You have to turn the page. If you keep moving forward, being your best in spite of what didn't work out, in spite of who did you wrong, you'll come into another chapter that has a sudden increase of God's favor. You'll come into a chapter where the light comes bursting in, where the God who is a very present help in times of trouble doesn't just show

61

up, He shows out. He does more than you can imagine. One day you'll look back and say, "God, I didn't like it, but without that difficulty I wouldn't have seen the new house, the promotion, or the new level. Joy came in the morning."

A PRAYER FOR TODAY

Father, thank You that in times of trouble, in times of weeping, when I don't see the way out, I can know that it's only for a night, for a chapter of my life. You will come bursting in with light and help. I believe that I have Your favor, and as I turn the page, joy will come. In Jesus' name. Amen.

HAVE DEEP ROOTS

When the ground is saturated, even a big sturdy oak tree with an extensive root system that extends beyond its canopy can be blown over by high winds. That's because most of its roots are less than twelve inches deep and don't have anything to anchor to.

It's the same principle in life. We all have things that come against us—a medical issue, a business downturn, a child getting in trouble. What's going to determine whether or not you stand strong and outlast these storms is the depth of your roots. The reason some people are always upset, offended, and discouraged is that they only have surface roots. They're moved by what somebody said or did or something unfair. They're always being tossed to and fro. But when you have deep roots, when you know that God is in control, you're not moved by what doesn't go your way. The winds may blow, but you're still standing.

A PRAYER FOR TODAY

Father, thank You for giving me the promise that because my roots are in You, I will not be moved. Help me to sink my roots of faith deeper in You and to trust in Your faithfulness. I declare that I am strong in You and in the power of Your might. In Jesus' name. Amen.

How great is the goodness you have stored up for those who fear you. You lavish it on those who come to you for protection, blessing them before the watching world.

PSALM 31:19 NLT

HOW GREAT IS HIS GOODNESS

King David said, "What would have happened to me if I had not believed to see the goodness of God?" I wonder how many blessings we're missing out on, how much favor, how much increase we're not seeing simply because we're not expecting it. We're not releasing our faith.

Right now there are blessings that have your name on them. There is promotion stored up, healing stored up, vindication stored up, a house stored up. God has already destined them to be yours. But if you think, *I'll never get married. I'll never pay off my house. I've made too many mistakes. God would never bless me*, that is going to keep you from God's best. Why don't you try a different approach and say, "God, I believe You have some surprises in my future. I believe I'll see Your goodness in a new way." When you live with this expectancy, that's when God will give you something to talk about.

A PRAYER FOR TODAY

Father, thank You for Your goodness and the many blessings You have stored up for me. Thank You that when I keep You first place and honor You, blessings will chase me down and overtake me. I believe You have some surprises in my future that will be fun to talk about. In Jesus' name. Amen.

INNER ALARMS

Sometimes you feel an unrest and uneasiness, like an inner alarm telling you not to do something, to stay away from a person, a situation, or a business deal. Everything may seem okay, but don't go against the still small voice inside. God sees problems that we can't see. He knows the people who are going to pull us off course. If that whisper is saying, "Back off," it's because God is protecting you. When you have big decisions to make, it's important to get quiet and listen to the whisper, listen to what you're feeling. You can't hear it if you're always busy, noisy, stressed out, getting opinions from others.

It's not that God isn't speaking; it's that you need times of quiet so you can hear the whisper.

Every morning I like to start the day off saying, "God, help my spiritual ears to be sensitive to Your voice today. Help me to hear what the Holy Spirit is saying to me." The more sensitive we are to the Spirit's whispers, to His promptings, the further we're going to go.

A PRAYER FOR TODAY

Father, thank You for all the ways You have protected me from harm and mistakes. Thank You that You haven't left me on my own to work out my destiny. Help my spiritual ears to be sensitive to what Your Spirit is saying today. In Jesus' name. Amen.

LACKING NOTHING

So often we think, *If I had more money and more talent,*
I could do something great. If I had a bigger house, I'd be
happy. But as long as you feel as though you don't have
enough, you'll make excuses to be less than your best.
You have to get a new perspective. God has given you
exactly what you need for the season you're in. You have
the talent, the friends, the connections, the resources,
and the experience you need for right now.

Psalm 34 says that because your trust is in the Lord,
He will make sure you have whatever you need when you
need it. You won't "lack any good thing." This means that
if you don't have it right now, you don't need it right now.

Our attitude should be: *I'm equipped, empowered, and anointed for this moment. I am not lacking, shortchanged, inadequate, missing out, or less-than. I have what I need for today.*

A PRAYER FOR TODAY

Father, thank You for the assurance that You have provided me with exactly what I need for the season I am in. I believe that You have equipped and empowered me with every good thing right now, and You will keep providing for me as I need it. In Jesus' name. Amen.

THE POWER OF "I AM"

Whether you realize it or not, all through the day the power of "I am" is at work in your life, for whatever follows those two simple words will always come looking for you. When you say, "I am so unlucky," you're inviting disappointments. "I am so overweight." Calories come looking for you. It's as though you're giving them permission to be in your life. That's why you have to be careful what follows the "I am" and not let it wield its power against you.

The good news is, you get to choose what follows the "I am." Get up in the morning and invite good things into your life. "I am blessed. I am strong. I am talented.

71

I am wise. I am disciplined. I am focused. I am prosperous." When you talk like that, talent gets summoned by Almighty God: "Go find that person." Health, strength, abundance, and discipline start heading your way, and it costs you nothing!

A PRAYER FOR TODAY

Father, thank You that my words have creative power and that I can use the power of "I am" to become who You say I am. Thank You that You call me a masterpiece and Your treasured possession. I will use my words to invite good things into my life. In Jesus' name. Amen.

DON'T HIDE

In Genesis 3, after Adam and Eve fell into sin, when God came looking for them in the garden, they hid in fear and shame. Sometimes when we sense that God is looking for us, we think, *I don't want God to find me. I'm ashamed of my weaknesses and sins. I already feel condemned enough.* This is where we mistake who God really is, as though He's waiting for us to make a mistake, ready to push us down even further.

But God is not coming to condemn you. He's coming to rescue and restore you. He wants to give you all that belongs to you as His child—the freedom, the joy, the peace, the victory, the abundance. Jesus says He came "to set at liberty them that are bruised" (Luke 4:18 KJV). When you're bruised by life, when you're hurt, it's easy to feel sorry for yourself and hide. God is looking for you to set you free, to heal you of your hurts, and to make you whole again. Step out into the light and meet Him.

A PRAYER FOR TODAY

Father, thank You that You didn't create me to hide my faults and weaknesses or to hide from You. Thank You that I can come to You and unload all the weight of heaviness, regrets, and feelings of unworthiness. I believe that You are setting me free and restoring me to wholeness. In Jesus' name. Amen.

THE MOST HIGH
SEES IT ALL

David spent long seasons of his life being treated unfairly by his father and brothers, by King Saul, by one enemy after another, and even by his own son Absalom. How did he keep such a good attitude and not get bitter? He just kept doing the right thing when facing malice, lies, and scorn. Deep down David understood this principle: "I don't understand why so much comes against me, but I know that the Most High God sees it all and He will not be silent. I know a reversal is on the way, that I will be vindicated, and that what God put in my heart will come to pass."

As David did, you have to stay faithful in the silent seasons. Stay faithful when you're in the shepherds' fields, being your best but being overlooked. People may not see you, but God sees you. He's the One who matters. He controls the universe. He opens doors no enemy can shut. One shift, and you'll go from being overlooked to being celebrated, from being discounted to being honored.

A PRAYER FOR TODAY

Father, thank You that You see everything that has happened to me, every unfair thing. Thank You that I can let go of it and forgive quickly before bitterness can come in. I declare that You are my vindicator and You will make my wrongs right. In Jesus' name. Amen.

*Let them say continually, "Let the LORD
be magnified, who has pleasure in
the prosperity of His servant."*

PSALM 35:27 NKJV

HAVE AN ABUNDANT MENTALITY

God's people were supposed to go around constantly saying, "God takes pleasure in prospering me." It was to help them develop an abundant mentality. Your life is moving toward what you're constantly thinking about. If you're always thinking thoughts of lack, not enough, and struggle, you're moving toward the wrong things. All through the day, meditate on these thoughts: *overflow, abundance, God takes pleasure in prospering me.*

God can make things happen that you could never make happen. He's already placed abundance in your future. Don't you dare settle in a place of lack and not enough. That is where you are; it is not who you are. That is your location; it's not your identity. You are a child of the Most High God. No matter what it looks like, have this abundant mentality. Keep reminding yourself, "God takes pleasure in prospering me. I am the head and never the tail."

A PRAYER FOR TODAY

Father, thank You that You take pleasure in providing for my prosperity and health and well-being. Thank You that You are my more-than-enough God and that I can ask You for big things today. I believe that You have already placed abundance in my future. In Jesus' name. Amen.

WONDER WORKING

We often pray for signs and wonders, but what if some of those wonders are in our kind words? What if the miracle is in something simple? What if telling someone that they're going to make it, telling your spouse every day that you love them, or giving your coworker or friend a compliment and encouraging them can work wonders? Don't discount the power of a kind word. One encouraging word can have an impact for a person's lifetime.

Your kind words can break strongholds in people's minds. Your encouragement can set their dreams into motion. Gifts will come out that they didn't know they had. Their passion will come back, and their faith will rise up. You have something that will not only nourish their soul like a medicine, soothe their emotions, and calm their fears, but your kind words bring healing to the body. God is counting on us to bring the nourishment. It seems ordinary to us, but to that person, it's something that will affect them for the good for years to come.

A PRAYER FOR TODAY

Father, thank You for the wonder-working power of words that can lift the heaviness off anxious hearts. Thank You that You have given me a gift that I can use to encourage others. Help me to use my words wisely and nourish hearts that need them. In Jesus' name. Amen.

Trust in the LORD and do good....
Take delight in the LORD, and he will give you
the desires of your heart. Commit your way
to the LORD; trust in him and he will do this.

PSALM 37:3–5 NIV

GOD-GIVEN DESIRES

Sometimes life can be confusing. There are so many different paths we can follow. We wonder, *How do I know what my purpose is? What am I supposed to do in this situation? Are the ideas and goals that I want to accomplish a part of God's plan? Should I pursue my desires? Are they a part of my destiny?*

In today's Scripture, David is saying that when you keep God first place, when you have a heart to please Him in all your ways, He will put the right desires in you. You can trust that your will, what you desire to do, will be aligned with His will. That means you can act on opportunities you feel good about, positions you want to take, or the person you're interested in, trusting that God is putting His desires in you. Knowing our purpose and God's will is not as difficult as we make it. There will be things that you're passionate about, things you're gifted at, opportunities that excite you, dreams that motivate you. That's God leading you into your destiny.

A PRAYER FOR TODAY

Father, thank You for the desires that You have put in my heart. Thank You that I can commit my ways to You, trust in You, and know that You will use what I am passionate about and my giftings to lead me down the right path for my life. I will delight myself in You and fill my mind with Your Word. In Jesus' name. Amen.

The steps of a good man are ordered by the LORD, and He delights in his way.

PSALM 37:23 NKJV

IS IT ORDERED OR DISORDERED?

Are you stressed over a problem? Losing sleep over a difficulty? Are you remembering that God is ordering your steps and that He knows what He's doing? Problems and difficulties serve a purpose. Would Joseph or David have made it to the throne without adversity? When you understand that there is promotion in every problem, you'll keep a good attitude. *God, I don't like this problem, but I know that You're ordering my steps. I'm going to come out stronger, promoted, better than I was before.* Sometimes the promotion means you've developed a greater trust in God. You saw His faithfulness, felt Him strengthening you and making a way where you didn't see a way. Your faith grew, your spiritual muscles got stronger, and your character was developed. Every time you come through a challenge, that's fuel for your faith. God is preparing you for greater things. The next time you face a problem like that, you'll think, *This is no big deal. He brought me through this in the past, and He'll take me through it now.*

A PRAYER FOR TODAY

Father, thank You that You order my steps in the way that is best for me and You delight in my way. Thank You that You have a purpose for every difficulty and promotion in every problem. I believe that You are strengthening me, developing my character, and preparing me for what's next. In Jesus' name. Amen.

He lifted me out of the slimy pit, out of the mud and mire; he set my feet on a rock and gave me a firm place to stand. He put a new song in my mouth, a hymn of praise to our God.

PSALM 40:2-3 NIV

BE A PIT PRAISER

When God sees you praising Him in the pit, praising Him in the storm, praising Him in the loss, that's what He calls "a sacrifice of praise." He knows it's not easy and you feel like quitting. When you praise Him in the pit, that moves Him in a greater way. It's one thing to be grateful when things are going your way, but when you have a song of praise in your heart when every circumstance says you should be depressed, get ready for God to show out in your life. David says in today's Scripture that praise brings you out of the pit. Praise when it's sunny, and praise when it's gloomy. Praise when business is up, and praise when it's down. David says in Psalm 34, "I will bless the Lord at all times. His praise will continually be in my mouth." God is looking for some pit praisers, people who praise no matter what happens.

A PRAYER FOR TODAY

Father, thank You that the pits I find myself in are only temporary stops along the way to my final destination. Thank You that I can offer You a sacrifice of praise because You hold victory in store for the upright. I believe that You'll get me to where I'm supposed to be. In Jesus' name. Amen.

Become wise by walking with the wise; hang out with fools and watch your life fall to pieces.

PROVERBS 13:20 MSG

WHO ARE YOU WALKING WITH?

It's important not only how we spend our time but with whom we spend it. The only thing that's keeping some people from a new level of their destiny is wrong friendships. You may have to prune off some relationships that are not adding value to your life. Don't hang around people who are not going anywhere, who have no goals or dreams, who compromise and take the easy way out. If you tolerate mediocrity, it will rub off on you. If you hang out with jealous, critical, unhappy people, you will end up jealous, critical, and unhappy. You cannot become who God created you to be hanging out with them.

Take a look at your friends. If your friends are winners, leaders, givers, and successful, if they have integrity and a spirit of excellence and are positive and motivated, those good qualities are going to rub off on you. Invest your time with them. They're making you better.

A PRAYER FOR TODAY

Father, thank You for the friends in my life who sharpen me, inspire me, encourage me, and push me forward. Help me to know if there are relationships that I need to prune and friendships that I need to be careful about. I want to walk with the right people. In Jesus' name. Amen.

By this I know that you delight in me:
my enemy will not shout in triumph over me.

PSALM 41:11 ESV

WHO'S ON
YOUR SIDE?

In today's Scripture, when David looked at where he was as the king and thought about all he had gone through to get there—King Saul trying to kill him, people betraying him, armies attacking him—he recognized that God was behind the scenes the whole time, not letting those enemies defeat him. It gave him a boldness, for he knew the Lord was on his side.

All of us have some of these "by this I know." When you look back at how you survived that sickness, how you put yourself through college, or how you broke that addiction, you realize it was only by the grace of God, and here you are. When you know the Lord is on your side, it gives you a boldness. You don't fall apart when opposition comes. Your attitude is: *You're messing with the wrong person. I may look ordinary, but I have a secret: the Most High God is on my side.*

A PRAYER FOR TODAY

Father, thank You for the history I have with You and for every time You have not allowed the enemy to triumph over me. Thank You for all the times You've shown me that You are at my side. By this I know that I will triumph. In Jesus' name. Amen.

Why, my soul, are you downcast? Why so disturbed within me? Put your hope in God, for I will yet praise him, my Savior and my God.

PSALM 42:5 NIV

GET YOUR HOPES UP

David had seen God's blessing and favor in amazing ways. You might think he'd never have a down period, but that's not the case. We're all tempted to be discouraged, to live defeated and not feel like going on. When we feel that way, we have to talk to ourselves as David did and say, "I am not going to let feelings rule my life or let these negative thoughts keep playing in my head. I'm getting my hopes up. God's plans for me are for good, and He will bring me out of this dry place."

You walked into the dry place, and the good news is that you can walk out. God didn't create you to go around dry, discouraged, and dragging through the day. He created you to enjoy life, not just endure it. There may be some things wrong in your life, but there's a lot more right than there is wrong. Start by being grateful for what's right in your life today and declare your hope in God.

A PRAYER FOR TODAY

Father, thank You for being the God who richly provides us with everything for our enjoyment. Help me shake off any of the blahs of this moment and fix my hope in You. I declare that I will be grateful for everything that is right in my life and give You praise. In Jesus' name. Amen.

WHAT'S ON YOUR THRONE?

When David faced Goliath, he never called him a giant. He called Goliath "an uncircumcised Philistine." David downplayed his size because he refused to put Goliath on the throne. He kept God on the throne. He said to Goliath, "You come against me with a sword and spear, but I come against you in the name of the Lord of hosts, the God of the armies of Israel."

You may be facing a giant of a problem. If you're not careful, you'll let that problem consume you with worry. The whole time God is in control and already has the solution, but you've taken God off the throne and put your problem on the throne. Here's the key: If God is not on the throne, you're not giving Him permission. God works where there's an attitude of faith. You can't have God and the problem on the throne at the same time. There's room for just one. Keep God on the throne.

A PRAYER FOR TODAY

Father, thank You for being on Your throne, for reigning as sovereign over my health, my finances, my family, and my circumstances. Thank You that You are my provider, my healer, my way maker, my deliverer. The throne of my life is reserved for You. In Jesus' name. Amen.

YOUNG AT HEART

No matter what age you are, you can be young at heart, full of faith and energy and creativity. Your spirit never ages. It doesn't have to get old and grouchy. You can stay young in spirit. The way that happens is to give no place to the negative. Get in a habit of emptying out any offenses, knowing that God is in control and will do what He promised despite what comes against you. Empty out the worry and anxiety. If you made a mistake, empty out the guilt. If you didn't do your best, empty out the regret. If you were upset because you didn't get the credit you deserved, empty out the self-pity. If you had a bad break and you don't understand why, empty out the questions. Don't try to figure it out.

If you get good at emptying out the negative every day, you'll be strong, vibrant, full of faith, and full of joy.

A PRAYER FOR TODAY

Father, thank You that I never need to get old in my heart and that I can stay young and vibrant in my spirit. Thank You that I can choose to empty out the worry and mistakes and offenses and let negative things go. Fill me with joy to overflowing. In Jesus' name. Amen.

God is our refuge and strength,
a very present help in trouble.

PSALM 46:1 NKJV

A VERY PRESENT HELP

In Acts 12, King Herod had killed the apostle James and chained Peter in prison between two guards. It appeared that Peter would be killed after his trial the next day. Herod had also set two guard posts at the big iron prison gate. Herod thought he controlled the gate and did his best to keep Peter from getting out, but he didn't realize that God was Peter's doorkeeper. He didn't realize that he couldn't keep God from coming in. God is a very present help in trouble.

While Peter was sleeping in the middle of the night, an angel showed up, shook him awake, and led him supernaturally past all of Herod's restraints. Notice how

God comes into the dark places. He comes with you into the prison, into the hospital, into the difficulty of a friend's betrayal. He comes when you're hurting, when you're lonely, when life is not fair. You couldn't get to Him, but God comes to you. He's with you right now, and He knows how to bring you out. Just trust your doorkeeper.

A PRAYER FOR TODAY

Father, thank You that You are my refuge and strength, the God who comes into the times when things in my life are not fair. Thank You that when I am hurting, lonely, or in a season of sickness, You will show out that You are my Lord. I believe that You are my very present help in any time of trouble. In Jesus' name. Amen.

STAY AT PEACE

It's easy to live frustrated because somebody is not doing what we want, discouraged because of a disappointment, upset because our dreams haven't come to pass. But God doesn't remove every frustration. He doesn't change every person we don't like or take away everything that's bothering us. When He says, "Be still, and know that I am God," this implies that if we're not still, if we're upset, frustrated, and worried, we're not going to know that He is God. Most of the times when we're frustrated, we're trying to change things that only God can change. We're trying to be God and fix things over which we have no control. You can't make people do what's right or make yourself get well. If you're trying to control everything, you're going to be frustrated. Do what you can, then turn it over to God and let Him take care of the rest. Stay at peace, knowing He's in control.

A PRAYER FOR TODAY

Father, thank You that I can be still and know that You are God. Help me to stop trying to change what only You can change and stop trying to fix things over which I have no control. I declare that I'm going to stay in peace and know that You are in control. In Jesus' name. Amen.

TIMES OF TROUBLE

In today's Scripture, God didn't say, "Trust Me, and I'll keep you from trouble. Trust Me, and you won't have any difficulties." He says, "Trust Me when you're in trouble, when things don't make sense, when the medical report is not good, when a loved one doesn't make it." If you trust God, He says, "I will rescue you and you will give Me glory." God is not going to leave you in the trouble, the heartache, or the dysfunction. That is not how your story ends. Don't believe the lies that say it's permanent. God will rescue you and turn things around. Chains that have held you back will be broken. You're about to see sudden breakthroughs, healings, promotions. You're on the verge of seeing God show out in your life. Keep believing, keep praying, keep expecting. Keep doing the right thing, having an attitude of faith, and your time will come. You're going to see the faithfulness of God. It's going to be unusual and uncommon. You couldn't make it happen, but you will know it's the hand of God.

A PRAYER FOR TODAY

Father, thank You that in times of trouble I have Your promise that You will rescue me and give me glory. Thank You that this season is only for a chapter of my life, and it's not how my story ends. I declare that I will trust You in times of trouble, when it's not happening my way, and when things don't make sense. In Jesus' name. Amen.

LIFE-GIVING WORDS

Many people have wounds from the past, wounds from people saying hurtful, judgmental words about them. We have something to offer them. Our words can help heal the hurts and break the chains that are holding them back. Our words have the power to lift people up, to help them get through a challenge, to push them toward their destiny.

When you tell someone, "I love you," you're not just being kind; those are healing words. It might be just a simple word of encouragement or a compliment, such as "I'm praying for you" or "You look great today." It's no big deal to you, but to them it helps heal a wound. It lifts their spirit, causing them to believe in themselves. Just letting people know that you care does more than you imagine. You have the power to put someone on their feet, to keep them from falling into depression, to cause them to pursue their dream.

A PRAYER FOR TODAY

Father, thank You that You have given me the power of words to lift others up. All through the day help me to speak kind words, offer compliments, give encouragement, and lift up those around me. I believe that as I lift others, You will lift me. In Jesus' name. Amen.

HAVE A CLEAN HEART

Psalm 51 is a prayer of repentance in which David acknowledged a sin he had covered up. His first step was to accept responsibility. You can't overcome what you don't confront—a hidden addiction, a failure, a hurt. When you hide things, it's going to eat away at you like a poison. David went on to say that God requires truth in our inner parts. You can't pretend and have God's blessing at the same time.

If you're covering something up, it's not going to go away magically. When you come to God and ask for His forgiveness and mercy, He'll begin to restore and put you back on the path to your destiny. David says, "Create in me a clean heart, O God. Restore to me the joy of my salvation." He got it out in the open, asked for forgiveness—and that was the turning point. God forgave and restored him, and David went on to do great things.

A PRAYER FOR TODAY

Father, thank You for Your unfailing love and great compassion that blot out the stain of my sins. Thank You that I can come to You for forgiveness and mercy and for truth in my heart. I ask for a clean heart and to walk in the joy of my salvation. In Jesus' name. Amen.

*Cast your burden upon the LORD,
and He shall sustain you; He shall never
permit the righteous to be moved.*

PSALM 55:22 NKJV

CARRYING OR CARRIED?

During the forty years when the Israelites wandered in the desert, at times they worshipped idols, large statues cut out of stone. As they traveled, they had to carry these heavy, burdensome gods. They carried their gods instead of letting God carry and sustain them. We may not make stone idols today, but sometimes we're carrying heavy burdens and troubles, trying to fix it all in our own strength. In a sense, we're carrying our god.

Are you letting God carry you? If you release your burden to Him and quit worrying and trying to figure it all out, He will carry you. God works where there's faith. If you're living stressed out, God steps back. You're not going to tap into the peace, the strength, and the favor that belongs to you. Don't carry those burdens. God is in the carrying business. When He carries your burdens, you don't have to carry them. All the burdens, stress, worries—release that weight. Let Him be God. You'll see Him carry you through things that you never thought you could get through.

A PRAYER FOR TODAY

Father, thank You that You know all the burdens I am carrying. Thank You that I can come to You and cast all the weights of worry, regrets, and feelings of frustration upon You. I know You're in control, so I'm going to live this day in faith knowing that You are carrying me. In Jesus' name. Amen.

The very day I call for help, the tide
of battle turns. My enemies flee!
This one thing I know: God is for me!

PSALM 56:9 TLB

A MIRACLE PUT IN MOTION

You have things you're believing for—perhaps a dream to come to pass, your health to turn around, or to meet the right person. You've been praying for a long time, but you don't see anything happening. It seems like God is on vacation and as though your prayers aren't doing any good. But what you can't see is that God is at work behind the scenes. Don't believe the lies that say your praying, believing, and standing in faith are a waste of time. He not only heard your prayer, but He put the miracle in motion. In today's Scripture, the psalmist says it happens the very day you call for help. In the unseen realm, God begins to change things in your favor. Just because you don't see anything happening doesn't mean the answer is not on the way. The people who see breakthroughs and promises fulfilled are the people who keep praying, keep believing, keep standing in faith.

A PRAYER FOR TODAY

Father, thank You that You never take vacations and that You hear every prayer and see me standing in faith. Thank You that in the unseen realm You have put a miracle in motion for me. I believe and declare that the answer is on the way. In Jesus' name. Amen.

WHAT IS FILLING
YOUR MIND?

Our eyes and ears are the gateway to our soul. What we watch and listen to and who we associate with are constantly feeding us. If you watch things that are unwholesome, listen to things that drag you down, and associate with people who are negative and gossip, you are feeding trash to your inner man. You can't be strong in the Lord and become all God created you to be with a diet like that. You are what you eat.

Today more than ever, we have the opportunity to feed on wrong things. There are hundreds of channels on television, countless websites on the Internet and smart-phones, music, movies, and video games trying to influence us. Take inventory of what you are watching and listening to. What kind of values is it portraying? Is it wholesome, inspiring you to be better and building you up? If not, make the necessary changes. Don't fill your mind and spirit with trash.

A PRAYER FOR TODAY

Father, thank You for providing me with Your Word as well as such an abundance of anointed messages, praise music, great books, and devotionals to feed my soul. Help me to be wise and disciplined to watch and listen to only what inspires me to be better. In Jesus' name. Amen.

*Through God we will do valiantly, for it is
He who shall tread down our enemies.*

PSALM 60:12 NKJV

SOMETHING AMAZING

Are you facing big challenges today? God doesn't send big problems to people with small futures. The bigger the challenge, the bigger the promotion. God gave David a nine-foot-tall giant problem in Goliath even though he was small and had no military training or experience. But David's valiant defeat of the champion of the Philistine army led to the throne. The size of your problem is an indication of the size of your future. The enemy wouldn't be fighting you so hard if he didn't know something amazing was in front of you.

Don't be discouraged because you have big challenges. Have a new perspective. God has something big in your future—big breakthroughs, big opportunities, big victories. If you could see the promotion on the other side of those problems, if you could see the healing, the favor, the fulfillment, you wouldn't be discouraged. You would go through that difficulty in faith, praising when you could be complaining, thanking God that He's fighting your battles. It's all a setup for new levels of your destiny.

A PRAYER FOR TODAY

Father, thank You that I am not on my own, I am not weak, and I am equipped for whatever I am facing. Thank You that You are with me, and that adversity is only a sign that You are about to do something amazing. I believe that through You I will do valiantly and come through in victory. In Jesus' name. Amen.

TODAY'S SCRIPTURE

*From the ends of the earth I call to you,
I call as my heart grows faint; lead me
to the rock that is higher than I.*

PSALM 61:2 NIV

TAKEN HIGHER

Many people get frustrated and soured on life because of their unanswered whys. Not everything along your life's way is going to make sense. You may never understand why something happened the way it did, but God knows what He's doing. He wouldn't allow it if it weren't going to somehow work for your good. This is where faith comes in. Nothing that's happened to you can keep you from your destiny. The only thing that can stop you is you. If you get negative and bitter and lose your passion, that's going to keep you from God's best. You may have had unfair things happen to you, but I've learned that the depth of our pain is an indication of the height of our future. The taller the building, the deeper the foundation. When you go through difficulties and unfair situations, God is getting you prepared to be taken higher than you ever imagined.

A PRAYER FOR TODAY

Father, thank You that You know best when it comes to the things I want and the twists of life that I don't understand. Thank You that You'll take me through my unanswered whys and lead me higher than I've ever imagined. I believe that Your plans for me are good. In Jesus' name. Amen.

UNCONDITIONAL TRUST

It's easy to trust God when things are going our way. But when our prayers aren't being answered the way we want, the problem isn't turning around, and we're not seeing favor, too often we get upset and ask, "God, why didn't You answer my prayers?" We think that when it changes, we'll be happy. Conditional trust says, "God, if You answer my prayers in the way I want and according to my timetable, I'll be my best."

The problem with conditional trust is that there will always be something that's not happening fast enough, something that doesn't work out the way we want. There will always be unanswered "why" questions. So are you mature enough to accept God's answers even when they're not what you were hoping for? God is sovereign. He knows what He's doing. You may not understand everything that happens, but God has your best interests at heart. It's not random. It's a part of His plan. Faith is trusting God when life doesn't make sense.

A PRAYER FOR TODAY

Father, thank You that You are sovereign and worthy of my unconditional trust. There are things in my life that I don't understand, situations I want to see changed, but even if things don't happen the way I hope, I'm still going to trust You. I believe You are in control. In Jesus' name. Amen.

EXCEEDINGLY ABUNDANTLY

You have plans, desires, and goals for your life, which is great. But keep in mind that God is directing your steps. In David's plan as he shepherded his father's sheep, he never thought he'd defeat a giant and become the king. In Nehemiah's plan as the cupbearer to the king of Persia, a thousand miles from Jerusalem, he never thought he would rebuild the walls of that city. In Esther's plan as an orphan growing up in exile, she never imagined she would become the queen of Persia and save the lives of her people.

You have your plans, but don't limit yourself. God's plans and ways are better than yours. He has exceedingly abundantly above and beyond plans in your future. Who knows where God is taking you? There are desires He's going to put in your heart that are going to boggle your mind. The beauty is that you won't be talked out of it. He'll make it strong enough to override the doubt, the naysayers, the fear, and you'll step into levels greater than you've ever imagined.

A PRAYER FOR TODAY

Father, thank You for loving me and having such an amazing plan for my life. Thank You that You promised You will do exceedingly abundantly above and beyond what I can imagine. I declare that You have never failed to be true to Your Word, and I look forward to how You will direct my steps. In Jesus' name. Amen.

We went through fire and water, but you brought us to a place of abundance.

PSALM 66:12 NIV

ABUNDANCE

When the enemy brings difficulties against you, it can seem as though things are out of control, as though you're in a fire or a flood, but don't believe that lie. God has you in the palms of His hands. Don't judge your situation too soon. Your time is coming. God has not forgotten about you. You're not doing life on your own. He sees you doing the right thing when it's hard and nobody is encouraging you. He sees you being good to people who are not good to you. He sees you enduring the hardship, not complaining.

Notice in today's Scripture that on the other side of the fire or flood is abundance. There's about to be a shift, a turnaround. You've been faithful in the fire, now you're about to see favor in the fire. On the other side of the flood of trouble, the breakup, or the loss is an abundance of joy, an abundance of strength, an abundance of resources. You're coming into great opportunities, great relationships, great fulfillment.

A PRAYER FOR TODAY

Father, thank You for how You bring me through the fire and water and into abundance. Thank You that You have me in the palms of Your hands and my time for abundance is coming. I declare that I will stay faithful and believe that greater is on the way. In Jesus' name. Amen.

TODAY'S SCRIPTURE

Praise the Lord; praise God our savior!
For each day he carries us in his arms.

PSALM 68:19 NLT

IN HIS ARMS

We all face seasons when we don't see how we're going to make it through. We lose a loved one, we're dealing with a sickness, or we have a child who's off course. It's easy to feel overwhelmed, to live worried and think we don't have the strength to go on. But David says that every day God carries us in His arms. You may have situations that you feel are too much for you, but God is saying, "Don't worry. I'm carrying you. You're going to feel supernatural strength, a peace that passes understanding, and favor that causes things to fall into place." On your own, you wouldn't make it through the sickness, the financial setback, the divorce, or the trouble at work, but you're not on your own. You're being carried by the God who created you.

God is protecting you, even when you don't realize it. He is moving the wrong people out of the way, opening doors that you can't open. You can rest in faith today, knowing that He has you in His arms.

A PRAYER FOR TODAY

Father, thank You that You are my Savior and the stronghold of my life, so I need not fear or be overwhelmed. When things come against me, help me to remember that You are carrying me in Your arms. I will rest in faith and peace today, knowing I am safe in my relationship with You. In Jesus' name. Amen.

*Those who hate me without cause outnumber
the hairs on my head. Many enemies try to
destroy me with lies...they make fun of me.
I am the favorite topic of town gossip.*

PSALM 69:4, 11–12 NLT

KEEP RIGHT ON
SMILING

What do you do when someone dislikes you without a
cause? They might not have even tried to get to know you,
but they judge you from a distance. Perhaps they don't
like you because you're successful, or you're a different
race, or you're happy. As David said in today's Scripture,
they attack you behind your back with lies, make fun,
belittle. These are tests we all have to pass. Are you going
to get offended and try to set them straight? Don't take
that bait. Stay on the high road. They're a distraction,

trying to get you to waste your time on something that's not between you and your destiny.

One of the best things you can do is ignore it. David went on to say, "But I keep right on praying to You." He was saying, "I don't give them the time of day. I just keep on praising, keep on smiling, and keep on running my race."

A PRAYER FOR TODAY

Father, thank You that I can be still and know that You are God, the Most High God, when I come under personal attack. Thank You that You are my great defender and my reputation is in Your hands. I'm going to relax and stay in peace. In Jesus' name. Amen.

QUIT LISTENING

It's easy to get drawn into conflict, baited into strife, when someone's goal is to get you stirred up. "Did you hear what so-and-so said about you? It's so wrong. You better do something about it." The best thing you can say is, "No, I didn't hear, and I don't want to hear. My ears are not garbage cans to fill with trash. They don't control my reputation. I am confident God will take care of it." Don't let people stir you up. Quit listening to the rumors, false accusations, and negative things people say. Keep that out of your spirit. Don't give it the time of day. People can't stop your destiny. It's a test. Are you going to get drawn into conflict and try to prove they're wrong? Or are you going to stay on the high road and let God fight your battles? People can say hurtful, negative things, but when you leave it in God's hands, there's a freedom. You can stay in peace, knowing that God is your defender, knowing that He's in charge of your reputation.

A PRAYER FOR TODAY

Father, thank You that You are the defender of my reputation and I don't have to listen to negative things people say about me. Give me wisdom to know when to keep my mouth closed and overlook something that bothers me. I recognize the destructive power of strife and give no place for it. In Jesus' name. Amen.

They did not remember his power and how
he rescued them from their enemies.
They did not remember his miraculous signs
in Egypt, his wonders on the plain of Zoan.

PSALM 78:42–43 NLT

DON'T FORGET

What has God done for you? Don't be like the Israelites who had seen amazing miracles and yet didn't remember them when they needed faith to move forward into the Promised Land. Those victories you experienced weren't just to protect you, to promote you, or to heal you. They're fuel. When you face new challenges, obstacles that look too big, if you remember what God has done, that's what will give you the faith, the confidence, the knowing that He's in control, that He has you in the palms of His hands. And whatever is trying to stop you will be silenced. The enemy may do his best, but his best will never be enough. The forces for you are greater than the forces against you. Don't be worried and afraid. Go back over your history. When you start thanking God for what He's done, faith will rise in your heart. You'll know that God did it for you back then, and He'll do it for you today.

A PRAYER FOR TODAY

Father, thank You for every time You have rescued me from an enemy and for the history I have with You. Thank You for the deep assurance in my heart that You are in control and that You will silence whatever is trying to stop me. I believe that You being for me is all that I need. In Jesus' name. Amen.

FILLED

It's easy to feel that you're limited by how you were raised or by what didn't work out in the past. Perhaps you don't have the training you feel you need, don't have the finances, don't have the connections. Sometimes good people in your life will try to convince you to accept mediocrity, to water down your dreams to match your present environment. But neither people nor your environment are your source. God is your source, and He is unlimited. Start looking to Him. He can take you from borrowing to lending, from addiction to freedom, from sickness to health, from lack to abundance. He says to open wide your mouth and He will fill it with whatever you need.

Victory starts in your mind. Abundance starts in your thinking. Don't let a limited mind-set keep you from the abundant life that belongs to you. Be a believer and not a doubter. Get rid of low expectations. When you get in agreement with God, angels go to work, miracles are set in motion, and healing, breakthroughs, and favor come looking for you.

A PRAYER FOR TODAY

Father, thank You for the promise that if I open my mouth wide, You will fill my life with good things. Thank You for being my source and for the way You always meet my needs. Help me to get in agreement with You and to be bold to ask You for the big things only You can make happen. In Jesus' name. Amen.

For the LORD God is a sun and shield; the LORD bestows favor and honor; no good thing does he withhold from those whose walk is blameless.

PSALM 84:11 NIV

IT'S CALLED "FAVOR"

What God has in your future can't be accomplished on your own. There are places He's going to take you that you can't get to by yourself. There will be obstacles that look too big, dreams that seem impossible. If it were only up to you, you'd get stuck. The good news is that God has bestowed on you something that gives you an advantage, that opens doors that you can't open, that makes you stand out in the crowd. It's called "favor." Favor will cause good breaks to come to you that you don't deserve. You weren't next in line, but you got the promotion. That's the favor of God.

You've been faithful, honoring God. Get ready for favor. Get ready for an explosive blessing. God is about to do something unusual, something that you've never seen, promotion that you didn't work for, and good breaks that you didn't deserve. You can't explain it or take credit for it. It's the favor of God.

A PRAYER FOR TODAY

Father, thank You that Your favor has been upon my life in so many ways. Thank You for the countless things You've made happen for my good that I could never make happen. I am getting ready for explosive blessings that are gifts of Your favor that I don't deserve. In Jesus' name. Amen.

SPEAK TO YOUR MOUNTAIN

The words you speak can be helpful like electricity. Used the right way, electricity powers all kinds of good things. But electricity used the wrong way can harm or even kill you. It's the same way with our words. Whether we speak positive or negative words, we will reap what we sow. If you're always speaking words of defeat and failure, you're going to live in a pretty miserable world. Use your words to change your negative situations and fill them with life.

The Scripture clearly tells us to speak to our mountains. Maybe your mountain is a sickness, or a college debt, or a floundering business. Whatever your mountain is, speak to that obstacle. The Scripture also says, "Let the weak say, 'I am strong!'" (Joel 3:10 NKJV). Start calling yourself healed, happy, whole, blessed, and prosperous. God is a miracle-working God. Stop talking to God about how big your mountains are, and start talking to your mountains about how big your God is.

A PRAYER FOR TODAY

Father, thank You for the creative power that You give my words to change my life. Help me to give my faith a voice by speaking words of life and blessing over myself and my future daily. I declare that You are greater than any mountain I face. In Jesus' name. Amen.

TODAY'S SCRIPTURE

Who is like you, LORD God Almighty?
You, LORD, are mighty, and your
faithfulness surrounds you.

PSALM 89:8 NIV

HE IS WHO HE IS

When you pray for something and then talk about how it's probably not going to happen, it doesn't do any good. Don't cancel out your prayer with negative talk. You can't pray for victory and talk defeat. You have to believe that you receive what you ask for, that it already happened. It's not, "I hope it's going to work out." There's a knowing. Your attitude is: *It's already done. Things have shifted in my favor.*

This is the confidence we can have in our God. He's called El Shaddai, the God of more than enough. He's called Jehovah Jireh, the Lord our provider. He's called

Jehovah Rapha, the Lord our healer. He's called the Great I Am, the all-sufficient One. When we ask in faith, when we receive it in our spirit, we can be confident that in the unseen realm our God goes to work. It's not "I wonder if it's going to happen." No, it's "When is it going to happen? I am confident in the God we serve, that He is faithful, that what He started, He will finish."

A PRAYER FOR TODAY

Father, thank You that You are the Most High God, El Shaddai, Jehovah Jireh, Jehovah Rapha, the Great I Am. I worship You, the Lord God Almighty, and I declare that there is no one like You. I will not cancel out my prayers by doubting Your ability to answer them. In Jesus' name. Amen.

TODAY'S SCRIPTURE

*He who dwells in the secret place of
the Most High shall abide under
the shadow of the Almighty.*

PSALM 91:1 NKJV

THE SECRET PLACE

Every one of us should have a secret place in our relationship with God, an inner sanctuary where we don't allow everything in. We guard our secret place against any worry, offense, bitterness, or trouble that may be happening on the outside. We don't let those into the inner sanctuary of our hearts. Our secret place should be a place of hope, of peace, of rest, of faith.

If you're allowing everything into your secret place—what they said, what didn't work out, the stress, the traffic, the hurt—it will become contaminated. When you allow negative things into your secret place, it will affect your attitude, your relationships, your vision, and you'll live feeling frustrated, upset, and worried. Quit giving negative things so much attention, reliving the hurt, thinking about the offense, dwelling on the disappointment. Don't bring that close to your heart. It doesn't belong in your secret place. The good news is, you control that door. You can't stop the storm around you, but you can stop the storm from getting in you.

A PRAYER FOR TODAY

Father, thank You that there is a secret place in my heart where You dwell and where I can abide in peace. Help me guard against all the negative things that try to get in and contaminate my peace and joy. I can't stop the storms around me, but I will stop the storms from getting in me. In Jesus' name. Amen.

*I will say to the LORD, "My refuge and my
fortress, my God, in whom I trust."
For he will deliver you from the snare of
the fowler and the deadly pestilence.*

PSALM 91:2–3 ESV

"I WILL SAY"

Notice the connection in today's Scripture between *I
will say* and *He will do*. It doesn't say, "I believe He is my
refuge." The psalmist went around declaring it, speaking
it out: "The Lord is my refuge." Notice what happened.
God became his refuge and strength. God was saying,
in effect, "If you're bold enough to speak it, I'm bold
enough to do it."

Have you ever declared that your dreams are coming
to pass? Have you ever said, "I will pay off my house"? "I
will start my own business." "I will get my degree." "I will

lose this weight." Whatever God has put in your heart, it needs to get into your conversation. Talk like it's going to happen. Talk like it's already on the way: "When I get married..." "When I graduate from college..." "When I see my family restored." Not *if* it's going to happen but *when* it's going to happen. That's your faith being released.

A PRAYER FOR TODAY

Father, thank You for being my refuge and my fortress, my God, in whom I trust. I speak it out loud because I know that it's true and I believe that You will deliver and protect me. Help me to release my faith and declare that my dreams are coming to pass. In Jesus' name. Amen.

Many are the plans in a person's heart,
but it is the LORD's purpose that prevails.

PROVERBS 19:21 NIV

CONNECTING THE DOTS

God sees the big picture. He knows how to connect the dots in your life to accomplish His purpose. You're never going to understand all that He's doing to prepare what He has for you. There will be times when He asks you to do something that makes you uncomfortable. You'll have to stretch, to push past the fear and uncertainty, and do what you know God is asking you to do. Every act of obedience leads to a blessing. You may not see it right now, but down the road God will connect the dots.

God's gentle whisper in your spirit may be telling you

to forgive, to let go of a hurt. That's uncomfortable. Your mind will say, "No, they hurt me too badly." You get to choose. Are you going to obey the loud, forceful, don't-change voice? No, let the gentle whisper be the voice you follow. It may be uncomfortable, but God knows what He's doing. When you're sensitive to the still small voice in your spirit, listening to His promptings, you're going down the best path for your life.

A PRAYER FOR TODAY

Father, thank You that You know what's best for me, and You're pushing, stretching, and enlarging me for a reason. Thank You that You will connect all the dots in my life to accomplish Your purpose. I believe that You will take every obedience on my part and bring great blessing. In Jesus' name. Amen.

LIKE A PALM TREE

The reason God said we'd flourish like a palm tree is that God knew we would go through difficult times. What's interesting about the palm tree is that when it is bent over by the strong winds during a hurricane, research shows that the extreme stretching is strengthening the root system and giving it new opportunities for growth. After the storm, when the palm tree straightens back up, it's actually stronger than it was before.

That's what God does for you when you go through difficult times. When you come out of the storm that was meant to defeat you, when you straighten back up, you're not going to be the same. You're going to be stronger, healthier, wiser, better off, and ready for new growth. God never brings you out the same. He makes the enemy pay for bringing the times of darkness and trouble. Your roots are going to be stronger. You're not only going to still be standing; you're going to be standing stronger.

A PRAYER FOR TODAY

Father, thank You for giving me the promise that because my roots are in You, I will flourish through the storms. Help me to sink my roots of faith deeper in You and trust in Your faithfulness. I declare that I am going to be standing stronger. In Jesus' name. Amen.

POWER TO REMAIN CALM

Don't be surprised if you find yourself in unfair situations where people don't keep their word, play politics and make you look bad, or betray you. Your flesh says, "Do to them what they did to you." It's a test. That's God seeing what you're made of. It's easy to tell people off and to be rude when someone's rude to you, but that will keep you at the same place. God wants to take you higher, to places you've never seen. He'll allow you to be uncomfortable. The Scripture calls it the fiery challenge that tests your quality. Sometimes God will put you in the middle of the fire. In that pressure, impurities will come out. Revenge—"Two can play at this game." Pride—"I don't have to put up with this." Sarcasm—"You really think you're so hot?" No, stay in peace. Let God fight your battles. The psalmist says God has given you the power to remain calm in times of adversity. That's passing the test. That's what allows God to take you where you've never dreamed.

A PRAYER FOR TODAY

Father, thank You that You have given me the power to keep calm in times of adversity. Help me to know the authority You have given me to rule over my thoughts, attitudes, and responses when people treat me wrong. I declare that I will not lose my cool in times of adversity. In Jesus' name. Amen.

ENTER WITH THANKSGIVING

What an amazing privilege we have to serve a personal God who desires a relationship with us. But notice that today's Scripture tells us that we shouldn't come empty-handed to the King of kings and the Lord of lords. What do we have to give that's worthy of Almighty God? Our praise. Our thanksgiving. Our worship. We should always enter His gates with an offering of thanksgiving from our heart.

Praise isn't just about singing songs in church. Praise is the expression of gratefulness to God for who He is and all that He has done. Praise gets God's attention. Praise is a powerful tool in our lives because God inhabits the praises of His people. When we enter His presence the right way, He enters our circumstances; and when God shows up, the enemy must flee. Today, enter into His gates with thanksgiving and open the door for Him to move on your behalf.

A PRAYER FOR TODAY

Father, thank You that I can come to You with a heart full of thanksgiving. I have so much to be grateful for because of Your goodness. You are good, and Your mercy endures forever! Thank You for doing exceedingly abundantly above all I could ever ask or imagine. In Jesus' name. Amen.

I will walk with integrity of heart within my house.

PSALM 101:2 ESV

BE A PERSON OF INTEGRITY

Solomon says, "A good name is worth more than great riches." Your reputation is one of the most valuable things you have, and it is built on the foundation of your personal integrity. A person of integrity does the right thing when no one is watching. You can have talent, determination, and vision, but without integrity you won't reach your full potential.

Where does it start? In today's Scripture, David was saying, "Starting in my private life, when I could compromise, give in to temptation, cheat people, instead I'm going to do the right thing. I'm going to be a person of excellence and show God that He can trust me." He went on to say, "I will not look at anything impure. I won't watch things that are going to poison me. I will not have anything to do with crooked dealings, things that are shady, not ethical." Your name is too important to let it become tarnished by not having integrity.

A PRAYER FOR TODAY

Father, thank You that down at the foundation of my life I can be a person of integrity, someone who's true to You no matter what. Thank You that as I honor You, You are a shield of protection to me. I will not let small things keep me from Your big blessings. In Jesus' name. Amen.

*Watch your tongue and keep your mouth shut,
and you will stay out of trouble.*

PROVERBS 21:23 NLT

KEEP YOUR MOUTH CLOSED

It's easy to let someone aggravate you and push your buttons, then use that as an excuse to be upset and say things you shouldn't. No, that's a test of your character. In that fire, impurities are coming out. Under pressure, you're seeing what's in you. It's also an opportunity to grow. You can change. You don't have to be sarcastic, to say hurtful, critical words that wound people and bring strife and conflict. Don't go year after year responding that same way.

One way to pass the test is really simple. Keep your

mouth closed. Quit letting your emotions control your mouth. Your tongue can destroy relationships, your tongue can get you fired, and your tongue can have you sleeping on the couch at night. The next time you feel like saying something hurtful or disrespectful, or telling someone off, take a deep breath, pause for ten seconds, and under your breath say, "God, help me to control my tongue. Help me to pass this test." Be the one to walk away from conflict.

A PRAYER FOR TODAY

Father, thank You that no matter how many times someone pushes my buttons, I can keep my mouth closed and stay out of trouble. Thank You that You are growing my character up and changing me. I will be the bigger person and be the first one to walk away from conflict. In Jesus' name. Amen.

TODAY'S SCRIPTURE

Praise the LORD, my soul, and forget not all his benefits—who forgives all your sins and heals all your diseases, who redeems your life from the pit and crowns you with love and compassion.

PSALM 103:2-4 NIV

NEVER FORGET HIS BENEFITS

When you look back over your life, consider some of the things you've faced that at the time you didn't think you could make it through. The obstacle was so large, the breakup hurt you so badly, the medical report was so negative. You didn't see a way, but God turned it around. He gave you strength to go on. That wasn't a coincidence. It was the hand of God.

Those challenges not only prepared you for your future, they've also given you a history with God. When

155

you're in a tough time, remember how God turned your health around or how He brought you out of trouble. When you remember how God has protected you, promoted you, healed you, and restored you, faith will rise in your heart. Instead of thinking, *I'll never get out of this problem*, you'll say with confidence, "God made a way for me in the past. He's going to make a way in the future."

A PRAYER FOR TODAY

Father, thank You that You are the Most High God and that Your hand has been at work in my life. Thank You for Your goodness and mercy that have been so evident in so many ways. I believe You are protecting me, promoting me, healing me, and restoring me. In Jesus' name. Amen.

TODAY'S SCRIPTURE

He allowed no one to oppress them; for their
sake he rebuked kings: "Do not touch
my anointed ones; do my prophets no harm."

PSALM 105:14–15 NIV

ANOINTED

There are times when people will try to make you look bad, say things behind your back, make little innuendoes about you. You can't stop that or make people do what's right, so don't waste time and energy on what you can't change. That's not your job; that's God's job. Your reputation is in His hands.

God says, "Do not touch My anointed." You are His anointed. He knows when someone is slandering you, mischaracterizing your motives, spreading rumors. You stay on the high road, and at the right time God will vindicate you. No one can defend you as our God can.

Don't let yourself sink down to their level. You always have to go down to engage with someone who gossips or who says things to demean others. Recognize who you're dealing with. That's not a person of integrity, someone who will believe the best, or who will be happy if you succeed. They will try to get you to join them in gossiping, finding fault, pulling people down. You're God's anointed. Stay up on that high level where you belong.

A PRAYER FOR TODAY

Father, thank You for the anointing You have put on my life. Thank You that no one can take that blessing from me, and that it is greater than whatever tries to stop me. I declare that You are my vindicator and I will not sink down from the high level You have me on. In Jesus' name. Amen.

SAY SO

Words have creative power. When you speak something out, you give life to what you're saying. For instance, it's important to believe that you're blessed. But when you say, "I am blessed," that's when blessings come looking for you. Today's Scripture doesn't say, "Let the redeemed think so, or believe so, or hope so." That's all good, but you have to take it one step further and *say so*. If you're going to go to the next level, to overcome an obstacle or break an addiction, you have to start declaring it.

When God created the worlds, nothing happened until He spoke. He said, "Let there be light," and light came. His thoughts didn't set it into motion; His words set it into motion. It's the same principle today. You can have big dreams, be standing on God's promises, but not see anything change until you speak. When you speak, good breaks, promotion, and ideas will track you down.

A PRAYER FOR TODAY

Father, thank You that when You created the worlds, You didn't just think or believe them into being. You spoke them into being. I believe that I am to speak out words that are true to Your Word and the faith in my heart, and that when I say so, You will act. In Jesus' name. Amen.

For he broke down their prison gates
of bronze; he cut apart their bars of iron.

PSALM 107:16 NLT

BREAKING DOWN GATES

You may have struggled with a sickness a long time. It looks as though the bronze gate to health has been locked, so to speak. I can see the lock breaking and the hinges moving. God's about to do something supernatural. That addiction, depression, or anxiety may seem permanent. Every thought tells you that you have to live with it, that you've been locked out of freedom. I can see the prison gate breaking into pieces. You're about to walk into wholeness. It seems as though you can't accomplish your dream, that you don't have the connections, that the loan didn't go through. It's like iron bars that will never move. I can see those bars of iron being cut in two. I can see God doing something unusual, uncommon. He's about to tear down some things that have been limiting you. Gates that look impossible are about to suddenly open—gates to healing, freedom, and promotion. When it's the right time, all the forces of darkness cannot stop what God has purposed for your life.

A PRAYER FOR TODAY

Father, thank You that You are the Most High God who breaks prison gates of bronze. Thank You that You are releasing me into freedom and that what has limited me in the past is not going to hinder me anymore. I believe that all the forces of darkness cannot stop what You are doing in my life. In Jesus' name. Amen.

A good name is more desirable than great riches;
to be esteemed is better than silver or gold.

PROVERBS 22:1 NIV

THE REWARD OF INTEGRITY

Your reputation is one of the most valuable things you have. You can have great riches and yet be despised, looked down on, and seen as shady. But when you're a person of integrity, other people say, "I can trust them. They always do the right thing. They're honest, fair, and consistent. They don't talk one way and live another way." Your name is too important to let it become tarnished by a lack of integrity. A life of integrity will take you much further than being dishonest and manipulative.

You can't fudge on your taxes or turn in an exaggerated expense account and expect God's favor. You may gain some material things, but you lose with God. He controls the universe. There's a lot we can get away with, hide, manipulate, and exaggerate. People may not see it, but God does. Anything you gain without integrity won't be what it should have been. Be honest. Be trustworthy. Be a person of your word.

A PRAYER FOR TODAY

Father, thank You that You are not limited to seeing me as other people see me. Thank You that You see my heart, and You know my faithfulness to You. Help me to live a life of integrity. I want my life to stand out as one who brings You praise. In Jesus' name. Amen.

But deal well with me, O Sovereign LORD,
for the sake of your own reputation! Rescue me
because you are so faithful and good.

PSALM 109:21 NLT

STAY SEATED

In Psalm 23, David says that God is preparing a table in the presence of your enemies. That means that in times when someone is coming against you, when false accusations come, rumors and slander, the best thing you can do is take a seat. Stay in peace. That's not the time to get defensive or show how you can play their game. Just imagine God preparing a feast, a celebration, with a seat there for you. God is going to honor and favor you in front of those who have talked negatively about you, disrespected you, and tried to push you down. God is going to vindicate you in public, so those who treated you the worst will see you promoted, honored, in positions of influence and respect.

Because you belong to the sovereign Lord, because you're His child, He will deal with you because of His reputation. It's not just who you are; it's whose you are. Now your part is to guard your heart, to not get offended, to not get distracted and join in battles that don't matter. Stay seated.

A PRAYER FOR TODAY

Father, thank You that You are the sovereign Lord who defends the reputation of all Your children. Help me to stay seated at the table You prepare for me in the presence of those who come against me. Let me not only see Your goodness but be used by You to show other people how great You are. In Jesus' name. Amen.

*When darkness overtakes him,
light will come bursting in.*

PSALM 112:4 TLB

LIGHT COMES
BURSTING IN

At times life may seem dark. You may not have the funds to pay your bills. Your medical report is not good. Maybe other problems seem insurmountable. We know that God is always with us, but the psalmist says that in times of difficulty, God is very present. You'll never see the fullness of who God is if you're in the light all the time. It's in the storms, in the difficulties, that God is most present. When you don't see a way out and it's dark, you're in prime position for God's light to come bursting in. It's going to happen suddenly—a burst of favor, of healing, of strength. You didn't see it coming. One moment you were struggling with debt and suddenly—one contract, one promotion, one good break—you have more than enough. What happened? The light came bursting in. The God who is a very present help in trouble said, "Your night season was only temporary. It's time for your breakthrough. Now it's time to propel you forward." God is about to do that for you.

A PRAYER FOR TODAY

Father, thank You that in times of trouble when I don't see the way out, and it's dark, that You come bursting in with light and direction. I believe that You, the Creator of the universe, have highly favored me and are about to propel me forward. In Jesus' name. Amen.

BE YOUR BEST TODAY

When we read about the heroes of faith, their lives seem so exciting, but the truth is, most of their days were routine. Moses experienced one miracle after another, but those involved only a few days of his life. Most of our days will be ordinary days, with some exciting days. If you live from big event to big event, waiting for something exciting to keep you encouraged, you're going to be disappointed.

Learn to enjoy where God has you right now. This is the day the Lord has made. It may be routine, but when you do the ordinary with a good attitude, that's getting you prepared for the new things God has in store. It's being faithful day in and day out, doing the right thing when the wrong thing is happening, staying in faith when you're not getting your way. You won't be promoted if you're not being your best where God has you right now.

A PRAYER FOR TODAY

Father, thank You for this day that You have made. Thank You that I can be faithful in the ordinary and routine, knowing that You are preparing me for the new things You have in store. I'm going to keep being my best, serving, giving, and loving right where I am. In Jesus' name. Amen.

HOW HONEST ARE YOU?

Today's Scripture is a powerful prayer. We have to be honest with ourselves. Sometimes we don't want to pray that. We want to keep things hidden. We don't want to deal with things that are uncomfortable, such as apologizing to someone we've offended. But it's much better to be open and honest. "God, show me areas where I need to change, not my spouse or my children. Show me where I need to come up higher."

When you live out of a place of humility and you're willing to deal with things that God brings to light, there's no limit to how high God will take you. We all have areas in which we need to grow, but it's tempting to make excuses, such as, "I've always been hot-tempered. I've always held grudges. I've always been critical, negative, arrogant, defensive. This is just who I am. Besides, they deserve it." No, you're running from the truth. You're comforting what you should be confronting. If you face those challenges, you'll step into a new level of your destiny.

A PRAYER FOR TODAY

Father, thank You that I don't have to hide my weaknesses, doubts, fears, or shortcomings. Search my heart and show me areas where I need to change and stop making excuses. I humbly admit that I don't have it all together, but I'm grateful that You're still working on me. In Jesus' name. Amen.

*For though the righteous fall
seven times, they rise again.*

PROVERBS 24:16 NIV

IT'S YOUR MOVE

We all go through disappointments, things that don't make sense—a friend walked out on us, we were overlooked for a promotion, we came down with an illness. You may have grown up in a home filled with abuse and dysfunction. The people who should have been loving to you were just the opposite. It's easy to let what's unfair be an excuse to not pursue your destiny. "I can't be successful. My company let me go." "I had a rough childhood. I'll never be happy."

Here's the key: It's not your fault that you got knocked down, but today's Scripture says it is your responsibility to get back up. It was wrong that they hurt you and walked away. It was unfair that you went through the injustice. That's not dismissing what you've been through or excusing their behavior. It's okay to feel hurt, to feel violated. God made us with feelings. But you have to get back up. Your move when unfair things happen is to go forward in faith, trusting that God will make it up to you.

A PRAYER FOR TODAY

Father, thank You that You are the Most High God, and because I am Your child, I have been made righteous through Jesus. Help me when I fall to never stay down in discouragement, hurt, or bitterness. I declare that I will get back up and move forward in faith. In Jesus' name. Amen.

My troubles turned out all for the best—
they forced me to learn from your textbook.

PSALM 119:71 MSG

FOR THE BEST

When you understand the principle that God is going to use difficulties for your best, life gets much more freeing. You don't get upset when things happen that you don't like. You know God allowed it, and He's going to use it for good. It's a part of the process. He may be developing patience in you. Whatever it is, He has a purpose for it. Keep the right perspective: It's all good.

We're not going to understand everything that does and doesn't happen in our lives, but God sees the big picture. He knows where the dead ends are, the shortcuts, the bumpy roads that are going to cause you heartache and pain. He'll keep doors closed that you prayed would open because He knows going through them would be a waste of your time. God is asking, "Do you trust Me with your closed doors and unanswered prayers?" He's getting you ready for the next level of your destiny.

A PRAYER FOR TODAY

Father, thank You that You know best when it comes to the things I want and ask You for. Thank You that You are directing my steps and that You'll take me through the things I don't understand. It may not all feel good, but I declare that it is all good. In Jesus' name. Amen.

STEP-BY-STEP

God has a detailed plan for your life. He knows your final destination and the best way to get you there. But God doesn't show you all the details. The Scripture says His Word is a lamp for your feet. A lamp implies you have enough light to see the life path in front of you but not for the next fifty years. If you trust Him and take that next step into the unknown, not knowing the outcome, He'll lead you step-by-step into your destiny.

The question is, will you be bold and take the next step that God gives you with the light you have? The unknown is where miracles happen, where you discover abilities you never knew you had, and where you'll accomplish more than you ever dreamed. If you have the courage to do what you know He's asking you to do, He has the provision, the favor, and all that you need to go to the next level.

A PRAYER FOR TODAY

Father, thank You that what lies ahead and is unknown to me is well known to You. I choose to rely on Your strength and Your Word that guides me step-by-step. I trust that You will go before me and take me to the next level. In Jesus' name. Amen.

YOU CONTROL THE DOORWAY

Studies show that we talk to ourselves up to thirty thousand times a day. There is always something playing in our minds. The Scripture tells us to meditate on God's promises. The word *meditate* means "to think about over and over." We need to pay attention to what we're meditating on.

Meditating involves the same principle as worrying. When you worry, you're just meditating on the wrong thing. You're using your faith in reverse. If you go through the day worried about your finances, worried about your family, and worried about your future because you're allowing the wrong thoughts to play, it's going to cause you to be anxious, fearful, negative, and discouraged. The whole problem is what you're choosing to meditate on. You control the doorway to your mind. When those negative thoughts come knocking, you don't have to answer the door. You can say, "No, thanks. I'm going to choose to meditate on what God says about me."

A PRAYER FOR TODAY

Father, thank You for giving me Your promises to meditate upon. Thank You that Your Word instructs me to think on things that are true and right, wholesome, pure, and of good report. I declare that my trust is in You alone and not in anything else. In Jesus' name. Amen.

When the LORD restored the fortunes of Zion, we were like those who dreamed. Our mouths were filled with laughter, our tongues with songs of joy.

PSALM 126:1–2 NIV

THE LAUGHTER OF AMAZEMENT

The Israelites had been taken into captivity by the Babylonians. The return and the restoration of Jerusalem had been anticipated so long that it seemed like a dream to them. Some of them had waited their entire lifetime. Their joy was beyond containment. They were laughing in amazement, saying, "This is like a dream. It's too good to be true."

Some of the things you've been dreaming about—to get out of debt, to start that business, to meet the right person, to finish college—the odds may be against you, it seems laughable, but God is about to surprise you. Stay in faith, because as with the Israelites, the day is coming when God will fill your mouth with the laughter of amazement. It's going to seem like a dream. You're not only going to be amazed, but the people around you are going to be so in awe that all they will be able to do is laugh with you.

A PRAYER FOR TODAY

Father, thank You for the things You've put into my heart that seem laughable and that I have to dare to believe can happen. Thank You that You do what seems too good to be true. I'm going to stay in faith and look forward to laughing in amazement. In Jesus' name. Amen.

Whoever has no rule over his own spirit is like a city broken down, without walls.

PROVERBS 25:28 NKJV

BUILD UP THE WALLS

When you let your feelings control you—anger, impatience, lust, a negative attitude—your walls of defense are down. The enemy can come in and run your life. God has given us self-control. Quit saying, "I can't stop it. It's too hard." You have the ability, but self-control is like a muscle—if you never discipline yourself to walk away when you feel like taking the easy way out, then your self-control muscle is very weak. You have to start exercising it by saying no to your flesh. You have a destiny to fulfill. But as long as you are controlled by these ordinary impulses, God can't release the amazing things He has in store for your future. Spiritual maturity has nothing to do with how many years you've been in church or how long you've known the Lord. It has everything to do with what kind of fruit you are displaying. Are you ruling over your emotions?

A PRAYER FOR TODAY

Father, thank You that You have given me the power of self-control to rule over my flesh. Thank You that I can discipline myself to do what's right and build up the walls of my character. I believe that as I exercise my self-control muscles, I will reach my highest potential. In Jesus' name. Amen.

TODAY'S SCRIPTURE

Blessed are all who fear the LORD, who walk in obedience to him. You will eat the fruit of your labor; blessings and prosperity will be yours.

PSALM 128:1–2 NIV

WHAT'S NONE OF YOUR BUSINESS

Someone has said, "What you think about me is none of my business." While people are free to think whatever they want about you, your part is to make it none of your business. You don't have time to worry about everyone else's opinion of you. You have a destiny to fulfill that is filled with blessings and prosperity. You have an assignment to accomplish through your obedience to God. It's not going to happen if you're image-driven, if you're making decisions based on other people's approval of you.

Don't let anyone sway you from what God puts in your heart. Don't waste another day trying to get their approval. You have a responsibility to become who He created you to be, not who someone else wants you to be. You don't need them to validate you; Almighty God has already approved you. When you come to the end of your life, He's simply going to ask, "Did you obey My Word and become who I created you to be, or did you let people squeeze you into their mold?"

A PRAYER FOR TODAY

Father, thank You that You have given me a destiny to fulfill and a life to be lived with purpose. Thank You that I have Your approval and that I can be free from trying to get other people's approval. I am going to walk in obedience to Your Word and become who You created me to be. In Jesus' name. Amen.

With a mighty hand and outstretched arm;
His love endures forever.

PSALM 136:12 NIV

NOTHING HAPPENS RANDOMLY

When you're tempted to get discouraged by the way your life is going, remember that you're not doing life on your own. God is behind the scenes orchestrating your life. God's strong hand and outstretched arm are not limited by the natural; He's supernatural. You can't see Him, but He's behind the scenes, and He controls the universe. He's working all things according to His will and for your good. When God is ready to promote you, He doesn't check with your supervisor. He opens the door. He controls what breaks come your way. Don't lose sleep over your boss or the people who are against you. His hand is over them. Don't get discouraged about your finances. He's about to bring promotion, opportunity, and increase that you didn't see coming.

What are you worrying about? The Most High God is maneuvering things in your favor. Live from a place of peace, knowing that nothing happens randomly. Your steps are divinely orchestrated.

A PRAYER FOR TODAY

Father, thank You for Your strong hand and outstretched arm in my life. Thank You for the open doors, the promotion, the healing, and the good breaks that You've already put in place to come my way. I believe that You are lovingly maneuvering things in my favor. In Jesus' name. Amen.

JUST ONE
GOOD BREAK

Sometimes we don't see how we can accomplish our dreams. We don't have the connections, the resources, the experience. It might not look as though it's going to happen, but what you don't realize is that you don't need a hundred things to go right—just one touch of God's favor and doors will open that you couldn't open. Just one good break, one right person, one phone call, one healing, one contract, and what seemed impossible will suddenly become possible.

Today's Scripture says the Lord will work out His

plans for your life. You don't have to work it out. You don't have to struggle and worry and try to fix every problem, straighten out every person who says something negative about you, and make things happen in your own strength. You can live from a place of peace, knowing that God has lined up the breaks you need. Get up every morning with the expectancy that He's going to surprise you with good things because His faithful love endures forever.

A PRAYER FOR TODAY

Father, thank You that just one good break, just one person, just one promotion, just one touch of Your favor can make the impossible suddenly become possible. Thank You that I can stay in peace and rest in Your faithful love. I believe that You are working out Your plan for my life. In Jesus' name. Amen.

TODAY'S SCRIPTURE

I praise you, for I am fearfully and wonderfully made. Wonderful are your works; my soul knows it very well.

PSALM 139:14 ESV

THE TRUE YOU

Inside every one of us is a blessed person who is confident, valuable, talented, disciplined. The Scripture says we are "fearfully and wonderfully made." The word *fearful* in the original language means "to stand in awe, to reverence." When God created you, He looked at you in awe and reverence. He calls you "a masterpiece." God didn't make anyone with a bunch of flaws. No, you've been exceptionally made.

But as we go through life, we make mistakes and develop bad habits. People do us wrong, shame comes, guilt comes, and insecurity. We feel condemned, not valuable. But underneath the failures, there's the true you, the one God created. The true you is the blessed you, the happy you, the successful you, the forgiving you, the confident you. It's still in you. The beauty of our God is that He never loses the vision of the true you or the reverence He felt when He created you. Despite the flaws and weaknesses, He still sees the masterpiece you are, and He'll keep making you into all He created you to be.

A PRAYER FOR TODAY

Father, thank You that You made me fearfully and wonderfully and in ways I have yet to discover. Thank You that You are working and molding me into the true me, the one You created me to be. I believe that the masterpiece in me will show out as I trust You. In Jesus' name. Amen.

PROTECT YOUR PEACE

Some people always have problems, always want your help, and are always in crisis mode. They expect you to come running, to cheer them up and keep them encouraged. And if you don't, they try to make you feel guilty. You love them, but you should put up a boundary to keep them from continually dumping their problems on you. You are not responsible for their happiness or to keep them fixed.

You have to protect your peace. You have a limited supply of emotional energy each day. If you're taking on their problems, you're not going to have the emotional energy for what you need. You're not their savior; they already have a Savior. Too often instead of helping them, we're simply enabling their dysfunction. If they get upset when you put up a boundary, they are controllers and manipulators. They like you for what you can do for them, not for who you are. You don't need "friends" like that. Make a change, and God will give you true friends.

A PRAYER FOR TODAY

Father, thank You that You have called me to love and help others but not to try to fix them or make them happy. Help me to protect my own emotional energy. I declare that I am not responsible for other people's happiness. In Jesus' name. Amen.

TODAY'S SCRIPTURE

You saw me before I was born. Every day of my life was recorded in your book. Every moment was laid out before a single day had passed.

PSALM 139:16 NLT

WRITE A NEW STORY

You may have gone through bad breaks and unfair things. The enemy would love to rewrite the story that God has already written about you. You have to take that pen back, cross out all those lies, and tell yourself a new story. God says He has beauty for those ashes, that He'll pay you back for the wrongs. Don't let circumstances, what didn't work out, or what you think you don't have convince you to live with the wrong story. Your story is setting the limits for your life. Don't tell yourself that you'll never be successful or get out of debt. Tell yourself a new story: "I'm made in the image of God. I'm crowned with favor. There is greatness in me. What I touch prospers and succeeds. Blessings are chasing me down." That's the story God has written about you.

Is your story contradicting God's story? Have you let people, circumstances, doubt, or negativity rewrite your story? Don't let someone else become the author. Take that pen back and write yourself a new story.

A PRAYER FOR TODAY

Father, thank You that even before I was born, You had recorded my story in Your book. Thank You that I can get my story in line with what You have already written about me in Your Word. I am going to make sure the pen stays in my hand and write a new story. In Jesus' name. Amen.

Teach me to do your will, for you are my God;
may your good Spirit lead me on level ground.

PSALM 143:9 NIV

LEVEL GROUND

When you're committed to living your life for God, you can know that the Holy Spirit is watching over and will be leading you on a level path for your life. Psalm 32 says, "I will guide you along the best pathway for your life. I will advise you and watch over you" (NLT). Notice how God takes you down the level path. When it comes to your purpose, to fulfilling your destiny, He is going to put the right desires in you to follow. He is going to advise you, instruct you, and watch over you. He's going to override wrong desires, close wrong doors, and move people out who shouldn't be there. You're not going to have to worry or wonder about which way you should go or what you should do. You can relax, knowing that God is not just opening the right doors and bringing the right people but giving you the want-to, the passion, the drive, and the wisdom to pursue your destiny. You can follow what He puts in your heart.

A PRAYER FOR TODAY

Father, thank You for being my God and for the ways that You are teaching me to do Your will. Thank You that Your Spirit is leading me down the best path for my life, putting right desires in my heart, watching over and advising me. I will walk confidently in Your ways. In Jesus' name. Amen.

TODAY'S SCRIPTURE

*Praise the LORD. Sing to the LORD a new song,
his praise in the assembly of his faithful people....
Let them praise his name with dancing and make
music to him with timbrel and harp.*

PSALM 149:1, 3 NIV

FREELY WORSHIP

In 2 Samuel, when David was returning the ark of the Lord to Jerusalem with shouts and the sound of trumpets, it says that "David danced before the Lord with all his might" (NLT). David was a respected leader, and he could have thought, *I need to be reserved, proper, and dignified. I can't let these people see me dancing and praising with all my might.* But David wasn't image-driven. He didn't live to gain other people's approval. He didn't run his worship through a filter of what people would think. Even when his wife said he looked foolish, he responded that he was dancing to the Lord, not to please people, and he wasn't about to stop.

There will always be people who try to put you in their box and convince you to be who they want you to be. If you're not strong, if you're focused on people's approval, you'll let their image of you become a reality. Don't let other people squeeze you into their mold, whether it's about how you worship or any other area. Sing your own song.

A PRAYER FOR TODAY

Father, thank You for the people You've placed in my life to help me move to my destiny. Help me, though, to not become dependent upon their approval or live with my image on the throne. I declare that I will freely worship and serve You with all my might. In Jesus' name. Amen.

ABOUT THE AUTHOR

JOEL OSTEEN is a *New York Times* bestselling author and the senior pastor of Lakewood Church in Houston, Texas. Millions connect daily with his inspirational messages through television, podcasts, Joel Osteen Radio on Sirius XM, and global digital platforms. To learn more, visit his website at JoelOsteen.com.

We Want to Hear from You!

Each week, I close our international television broadcast by giving the audience an opportunity to make Jesus the Lord of their lives. I'd like to extend that same opportunity to you. Are you at peace with God? A void exists in every person's heart that only God can fill. I'm not talking about joining a church or finding religion. I'm talking about finding life and peace and happiness. Would you pray with me today? Just say, "Lord Jesus, I repent of my sins. I ask You to come into my heart. I make You my Lord and Savior."

Friend, if you prayed that simple prayer, I believe you have been "born again." I encourage you to attend a good Bible-based church and keep God in first place in your life. For free information on how you can grow stronger in your spiritual life, please feel free to contact us.

Victoria and I love you, and we'll be praying for you. We're believing for God's best for you, that you will see your dreams come to pass. We'd love to hear from you!

To contact us, write to:

Joel and Victoria Osteen
PO Box #4271
Houston, TX 77210

Or you can reach us online at www.joelosteen.com.